DRUKHARI

THEY ARE THE PREY-TAKERS, THE BLADEMASTERS AND THE
FLESHCRAFTERS. THEY ARE THE SCHEMING, SELF-SERVING RAIDERS
OF A GALAXY FIT TO FULFIL THEIR HAUNTED PLEASURES. THESE
TORTURERS AND ENSLAVERS FEED A SICKENING SOUL-HUNGER WITH
THE PAIN AND FEAR OF OTHERS. THEY HUNT ON MOONLESS NIGHTS
AND CRAWL FROM POOLS OF SHADOW, ALL TO FEAST ON ANGUISH. PRAY
YOU ARE WORTHLESS ENOUGH TO BE IGNORED. PRAY YOU WILL SEE
THE DAWN'S LIGHT WITH INTACT EYES.
PRAY THEY DON'T TAKE YOU ALIVE.

CONTENTS

PRODUCED BY THE WARHAMMER STUDIO

With thanks to the Mournival and the Infinity Circuit for their additional playtesting services

INTRODUCTION

Welcome, galactic raider, to *Codex: Drukhari*. In your hands is a tome to entice and amuse your jaded passions. Inked upon its bound pages are revelations of the cruel drives of a decadent alien aristocracy, the depths to which these sadistic pirates gladly dove to survive and the ways in which they flourish, unhindered, in a fractured and fearful galaxy.

The Drukhari are a degenerate society of the ancient Aeldari xenos race. They are a dark culture of torturers and raiders, striking out at the galaxy's inhabitants from their labyrinthine shadow-realm of Commorragh. Selfish, prideful, arrogant and murderous, the Drukhari are a self-serving people. The militant syndicates of their Kabals, the hedonistic gladiatorial cliques known as Wych Cults and the Haemonculus Covens that operate gruesome guilds of arcane alchemists all vie with each other for power and material wealth. The Drukhari's fractured civilisation is held together with fear, intimidation and a horrific trade in pain and torment that feeds their withered souls. With advanced science they emerge from webway portals to raid with superior anti-grav vehicles, hideous vat-grown cyborgs and coteries of venom-shooting killers, all to secure yet more captives for their bloody arenas and vile laboratories.

The diverse range of Drukhari miniatures offers a fantastic array of options for both veteran hobbyists and newcomers alike. Just as the factions within Commorragh society ally and rupture in shifting collusions, your realspace raiding party on the tabletop might be made up of a mixture of forces. Conversely, they may concentrate solely on one or two armies to represent the warriors of a single, obsessed noble. Perhaps you prefer gang-like cartels made up of Kabalite Warriors and their ruling Archons, supported by attack craft such as Voidraven Bombers or the winged services of mercenary Scourges. Maybe the exotic arena fighters of the Wyches are more your style, leaping into battle from baroque, skimming transports and being accompanied to war by exotic beasts. Or perhaps your raiding party requires the surgical horror of the Haemonculi and their shambling creations, wielding toxin-coated blades.

However you put your Drukhari force together, they offer a satisfying painting experience for people of all abilities. The range offers myriad textures of smooth curves and angular armour panels, exposed flesh, barbed chains and flayed skin, not to mention the possibility of strange, alien creatures that fight for the Drukhari. These provide a rich palette that can be vividly brought to life in as simple or as complex a way as you prefer.

This Codex contains all the rich background, stunning imagery and evocative rules you need to put together your own realspace raiding party of Drukhari, along with photographs of stunningly painted examples to inspire your own creations. It also contains exciting Crusade content you can use to follow the sadistic careers of your arrogant warriors from one prey-world to the next, as they amass ever more power.

The toxic factions of the Drukhari are the most sadistic, decadent and vicious elements of a long-lost stellar empire. They occupy the splintered city-realm of Commorragh within the twilight domain of the ancient webway. From there, the Drukhari raid and plunder the myriad races of the galaxy.

The Drukhari are experts in precise torture, sharp blades, cruel poisons and eldritch abominations. Using the labyrinthine network of webway spars, they strike almost anywhere. Realspace raiding parties prey upon worlds across the galaxy, surging from hidden portals unknown to those they see merely as cattle or playthings.

To those they leave alive to spread fear of their passing, these arrogant xenos are evil incarnate. While the Drukhari's superior science has mastered a multitude of feats, it ultimately focuses on their victims' misery – how to create it and how to prolong it. Striking where they please, not for any resources their victims value, they come to inflict suffering and anguish only ingenious epicureans of torment could imagine. The agony of others fills an aching void within them, a cursed soul debt they must all pay.

And pay they do, with inordinate relish.

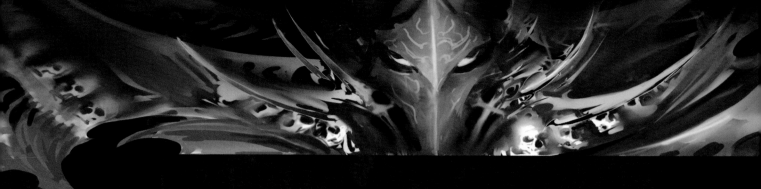

TWILIGHT RAIDERS

The Drukhari exemplify every obsessive and wanton act of cruelty that all Aeldari risk giving in to. They are a selfish breed of xenos raiders, seeking only their own twisted fulfilment at the expense of all others, even their own kind. In piratical forays of all sizes, the Drukhari prey upon the races of the fractured galaxy, revelling in the slaughter and fear they cause.

From the depths of their subdimensional realm – the Dark City of Commorragh – raiding parties of sadistic Drukhari gleefully strike out. They hunt for pleasure, and their pleasure is the pain and terror of the galaxy's races. For those unfortunates taken as captives, a drawn-out existence of agony and fear awaits, providing sport, amusement and spiritual sustenance for their captors. Little pleases the Drukhari more than the screams of their prey, the sight of horror in their victims' eyes or the feel of flesh parting under their blades. Every nuance of misery that the refined senses of the Aeldari can detect – the sight, sound and taste of suffering – is a potent narcotic that Drukhari raiders rapaciously consume.

The Drukhari are tall, slender and graceful in form, with natural athleticism, lithe strength and perceptive senses. Their long lives are artificially extended by gruesome means, enabling them to devote their piercing intellect across entire epochs to the mastering of singularly depraved obsessions. They are masters of many forms of close combat with hooks, blades and cruel lashes of countless types; in the deadly cut and thrust of acrobatic melee, their speed and dexterity make them lethal. A Drukhari's skill in close-quarters slaughter extends to each part of their body. Many of their varied castes of warriors wear a variety of close-fitting bodysuits or segmented armour, which afford incredible agility and often incorporate razor-sharp blades and barbs.

Drukhari science produces abominable poisons and haemotoxins, or elixirs made from the rendered down remains of their captives. In their eldritch forges are built superlative personal armaments as well as lightning-fast strike craft and anti-grav vehicles, which are fitted with monomolecular barbs and other weapons that inflict painful death in exotic ways.

REALSPACE RAIDERS

Raiding parties of Drukhari – forged through fractious alliances in Commorragh – attack planets, orbital habitats, fleets of ships and any other target that offers bounties of sentient beings. In blade-prowed transports, they often strike from above, appearing with no warning in order to stoke as much confusion and terror as possible. Drukhari technology is so far advanced that it is often viewed as mystical or magical by the races they prey upon. Their splinter weapons fire shards of crystalline substances laced with engineered venom, while other armaments defy any notions of physical laws known to the Imperium. Baroque, trophy-hung barges descend on jets, unleashing beams of darkness, nightmarish energies or psycho-empathic terror fields. Surgically augmented mercenaries and pain-adepts leap from their dark realm through shimmering portals, directly into the terrified presence of their prey, while ghastly horrors crawl from the shadows themselves.

Drukhari often attack as night falls, or their strange technology can even artificially generate such conditions, causing base fears to claw at their

victims' minds. Most realspace raids are convened to take captives – the raw fuel upon which Drukhari society thrives. Once brought to Commorragh, these unfortunates are hunted in vast arenas watched by thousands, experimented upon with vile surgeries and drugs, or are used fulfil any of the countless roles by which the Drukhari can profit off their suffering.

Even in raids with unusual and esoteric goals, such as the enacting of vengeance upon a rival, the execution of some murderous performance or the theft of an advanced artefact from their kin – the Aeldari of the Craftworlds – participation by the cruel citizens of Commorragh is highly sought. All Drukhari desire to sate a gnawing need at their heart to inflict pain wherever possible. If not against the other races of the galaxy, then readily upon other Drukhari within Commorragh.

THE DARK CITY

Commorragh is unlike any city of the Imperium. It is a twisted, fractured connection of sub-dimensions and satellite realms within the shifting webway of legend. Human captives brought into its environs cannot comprehend even the fraction they can see of the dark and shadowy landscape. A labyrinth of dark spires, crowded slums, starship docks and vast arenas – threaded through with streams of screaming captives and snarling beasts – overlays layers of hidden donjons, oubliettes and secret abodes. The temporal and spatial irregularities within the webway have allowed Commorragh to spread and branch like a tainted, crystalline fungus that reflects the society within. Cunning and powerful factions vie for prominence in a realm where piracy, murder, scheming and betrayal are facts of everyday life. Only the strong survive in Commorragh, and the Drukhari have had millennia to winnow out the weak.

A CONCENTRATION OF EVIL

No Aeldari would willingly risk travelling through the warp. There, the bright flare of their souls would attract the attention of the Chaos God Slaanesh, whom all Aeldari fear as 'She Who Thirsts'. Instead, they employ the webway's maze passages. At the centre of this inconceivably huge construct of astral nodes sits Commorragh.

The Dark City's mountain-sized spires house the ostentatious halls of the Drukhari elite. Beneath these crooked pinnacles cluster weapons shops and laboratories, moon-sized dockyards, the chambers of lesser lordlings, corkscrew skyways, sinister shrines and gladiatorial arenas. Encrusted about the foundations of the Dark City are a shifting morass of nightmare slums,

dead-end alleyways and predator-haunted hovels, while hanging like benighted fruit below are the sickening demesnes of fleshcrafters and arcanologists. Entire pocket dimensions are held together in deeper levels of existence by incomprehensible technologies. Gravity is applied where it is needed, cruelly wrought to suit the arrogant whims of those who master it. Stolen suns shine weakly in the firmament, orbited by captured planets and shoals of gutted starships, their crews long since prized out of every cranny. The impossible landscape of Commorragh is the result of millennia of boundless ambition and reckless expansion, and bears many scars of Drukhari hubris, such as the yawning maw known as Khaine's Gate, through which the denizens of the warp are able to pour into the Dark City.

THE GENESIS OF EVIL

More than ten millennia ago, the galaxy-spanning empire of the Aeldari came to a cataclysmic end in the race's Fall. Many of the splintered survivors of that apocalypse forged their own course of desperate existence from that time onwards, but the Drukhari can be said to have trodden their dark path for far longer, turning an established decadence into their salvation.

Any knowledge of xenos is brutally suppressed within the Imperium. Thus, only a fraction of Mankind's teeming trillions knows anything of the Aeldari's supposed history. Of these, most are high-ranking agents within the shadowy Ordo Xenos of the Inquisition. Some within this group are entrusted by Aeldari contacts with tales that claim to tell of the Fall of their race, yet the natural suspicion of Inquisitors leads them to view such data as disinformation, myth or, at best, apocalyptic metaphor. Nevertheless, they are tales that all Aeldari learn and that different strands of their race treat variously as cautionary tales of hubris, stories of ultimate betrayal and even accounts of the excision of weakness.

The ancient Aeldari empire existed as the most advanced and dominant race in the galaxy many millions of years ago. Through their science they created worlds and extinguished stars, while the unlimited potential of their psychic arts ensured that there was no force that could deny their authority. The technologies at their fingertips meant the Aeldari could live a life of leisure free from concepts of manual labour, able to pursue any diversions their powerful emotions and soaring intellect could conceive. Using the webway, they travelled between the stars of the galaxy in a heartbeat, delving into esoteric studies and unusual passions.

The long lifespan of the Aeldari led many to seek ever more extreme avenues of exploration as they tested the limits of their own psyches. The thoughts and emotions of their race can rise to heights of bliss or plumb dark nadirs of anguish that are unknown to Mankind. These extremes were reached for by many of an arrogant race that increasingly saw itself as far beyond any boundaries of morality. On many Aeldari worlds, cults of pleasure and pain, dabblers in extravagant technologies and lodges that consorted with narcotics distilled from across their pan-galactic empire sprang up.

The Aeldari had spread from the worlds at the heart of their civilisation to, not only countless other planets throughout the galaxy, but also within the webway itself. Nodal cities and mighty ports flourished within the interconnected network of misted passageways that led to Aeldari colonies far and wide. Some of the pleasure cults, among whose devotees were great numbers of the aristocratic nobility of Aeldari society, relocated into these webway settlements as they came under pressure to curb their excesses. Within these complex hubs, where shadowy trades in people and substances could be carried out secretly, many of them flourished.

The greatest of the webway's mighty port-cities was a vast metropolis known as Commorragh. Its unrivalled connections to countless portals ensured its value, and granted the city unprecedented autonomy to ensure that no one faction within the empire could deny its use to any other. Yet with lax regulation, Commorragh grew ever larger and became a home for every illicit and reprehensible pastime within the empire. The dilettante lords and ladies who headed many of the pleasure cults grew more powerful and, with both their influence and Commorragh's vast flows of shipping and connections, countless shadowy creeds spread to world after world.

The Aeldari's psychic souls flare brightly in the mirror realm of the warp. Powerful emotions in that dimension can take form, and the soaring highs and crushing lows of the psychically sensitive Aeldari began to coalesce. Quiescent ripples of agony and ecstasy echoed through time and space. The surging tides of the warp began to coil in a vortex around the constant stream of extreme sensation that flowed from the increasingly depraved society of the Aeldari. Around their emotions accreted a nascent entity of excess; content at first to wait and grow, it fed on the torrent of intensity put forth by the Aeldari while its dreams in turn seeped back to them, driving their vile exuberance to greater depths.

THE FALL

There were those in the Aeldari empire, among the spiralling insanities and obsessions pervading their people, who foresaw calamity. Some of the first to act were the Exodites, who left the decadent centres of civilisation behind to begin again on wilderness worlds far from the trappings of indulgence and excess. Much later, after incalculable efforts of psychic engineering, a movement of ascetic puritans departed on delicate planet-sized ships, bearing huge colonies through the void and into the depths of empty space. These were the craftworlds, and among those who fled upon them were many with the seer sight. They prophesied a terrifying and tragic horror ahead that echoed through time. Their warnings were scoffed at or ignored, and some of their number fell foul of the influential pleasure cults before they had chance to escape.

Freed of the appalled and doubting elements that had barely kept it in check, Aeldari society plunged deeper into lascivious decay. Towards the end, the streets of their ancient cities ran with blood. Star-spanning orgies of pleasure and unbridled violence accompanied clashing rhythms, dazzling sights and depraved crimes as the Aeldari tore one another apart in heady displays of cruelty. In truth, their race's decline had taken many millennia to congeal into this grotesque abomination of reality. When the end came, it was in a single, horrifying instant.

The Chaos God Slaanesh, the Dark Prince of Excess, was birthed in the roiling warp with a reality-shattering metaphysical roar. Its exultant psychic screams ruptured the veil between the warp and realspace. Hundreds of star systems at the heart of the Aeldari empire were rent apart and countless more swallowed whole. The greatest warp storm the galaxy had ever seen erupted in their place, a yawning tempest of madness thousands of light years across – that which Mankind would later call the Eye of Terror. In its first sucking intake of existence, Slaanesh drained the souls of almost the entire Aeldari race, gorging on the pain of billions upon billions in a single, gluttonous moment of excess. The resilient Aeldari psychic essences, capable of experiencing extremes, suffered an infinity of agony.

Very few Aeldari escaped this fate. Some of the Exodites and those aboard craftworlds – the forebears of the Asuryani – had managed to flee fast enough or far enough, but many of their number still perished. The Aeldari maintain that, during Slaanesh's birth, it even devoured most of their gods. As an empire, the Aeldari had ceased to be. As a species, a desperate struggle for survival has dominated their lives ever since.

The webway network, occupying its twilight site between the warp and realspace, suffered terribly from Slaanesh's arrival. Vast tracts were crushed or fractured, allowing the essence of the warp to pour in at many places, with daemons following greedily. Yet many dimensions and spars within the webway survived, and Commorragh itself remained unbreached. Multiple layers of psycho-crystalline defences sealed off tainted or damaged spars, while other sections mysteriously vanished, never to be seen again. Shielded by the ineffable nature of the webway, those within Commorragh survived Slaanesh's birth screams. In their supreme arrogance, they did not cease their quest for excess and selfish fulfilment, not even for a moment. Repentance, atonement or shame for what they surely must have understood could be traced, in part, to their own actions, were unknown concepts to a

people who acknowledged no limits on their ambition or power.

If the inhabitants of the webway port-city believed they had escaped without consequence, that they had evaded the Chaos God's immortal hunger, they were deluded. The echoes of Slaanesh's gluttony rippled throughout existence, and wrought insidious changes within the remaining Aeldari on Commorragh. They had not escaped the Fall of their race, though it was a long time before they realised it. Rather than having their sentient essence consumed by the Chaos God in one great draught, their souls were slowly draining away, drip by drip, into the warp. There, they were swallowed by Slaanesh, the abhorrent warp entity that haunts every Aeldari, and that they all know as 'She Who Thirsts'.

The remnants of their race fear Slaanesh, for the god of desire was born of their own dark obsessions and hungrily waits beyond the veil for them. They have a terror of dying that runs far deeper than the mere regret of life's ending. The Aeldari's strong psychic self can survive death, and while once their souls passed – they believe – into the realm of their own gods, now all that waits to feast upon them is Slaanesh. Different surviving strands of the Aeldari race discovered their own ways of avoiding this horror. The Aeldari of Commorragh – those who became the Drukhari and endured the aching seepage of their souls – found that others could suffer in their stead.

THE SOUL DEBT

Those who became the Drukhari had long preyed upon others, whether Aeldari or further sentient species. Now, they saw that stringing the moments of pain and terror out as agonisingly as possible replenished their waning spirits. Thus were born the Drukhari, as a new era of feverish torment and captive acquisition spread throughout Commorragh.

They became a race of sadistic parasites, feeding the yawning void within themselves by committing the most unspeakable acts of excruciation. Through their advanced technology, they devised ever more macabre ways of extracting suffering, with which they paid the soul

debt they would forever owe to She Who Thirsts. In their selfish and indulgent narcissism, they viewed other races – even other Aeldari – as weak beings deserving of contempt, and as chattel whom individual Drukhari had the right to abuse and discard for their own, dark ends.

The agony of others – savoured by the Drukhari's refined senses – nourished their withering souls, but while the curse could be abated, it could never be denied. The gnawing of Slaanesh's hunger clawed at the soul of every Drukhari, winnowing their spirit and vigour constantly. Every delicious nuance of terror, every sublime, nerve-shredding ounce of pain that they drank in from their victims, could only provide temporary succour from the unstoppable soul-sickness. Thus, the Drukhari sank into a spiralling mire of damnation and depravity.

Those who could not sate their need for anguish suffered a horrific withering of spirit. They became shadows of their former grandeur, desperately seeking any morbid sustenance. Fading to husks, these unfortunates weakened until they were prey for other pain-hungry Drukhari. Meanwhile, those who had recently fed on the most subtle and rare of agonies shone with a cold aura of vigour. Dull eyes regained their malicious gleam, and a supernatural potency invigorated their souls.

Raids into realspace multiplied as never before, seeking captives to satiate the Dark City's people. The countless pleasure cults, guilds, lodges and syndicates vied for power and patronage. Piratical fleets of ships spread out through the galaxy, herding millions of captives into the depths of Commorragh every day. The trade of prisoners and of expertise in misery and degradation blossomed like a dark flower.

To this day, Commorragh remains a canker of evil. The Drukhari raid from its dark portals to claim captives for gruesome ends. In many cultures, countless myths and dark fables warn of lean hunters with grasping hooks and hungry grins, who kill the fortunate with each caress, and take away those who are not…

THE RISE TO POWER

The depraved aristocracy of Commorragh, whose noble houses had risen to power through the various pleasure cults, are not the sole lords of the Dark City. Their complex web of intrigue, assassinations, gruesome commerce and debauched entertainments is held together by the supreme will of the Living Muse – Asdrubael Vect.

The most powerful individual in all of Drukhari society has countless epithets: The Lord of Darkness; the Supreme Overlord of Commorragh; the Living Muse; the Upstart Filthling. Asdrubael Vect's is the hand that moves the pieces in the insane geometries of conspiracies, favours and contracts that dominate Commorragh. He is feared, despised, fawned on – and perhaps even revered – by the shifting forces that control the city of horrors as he sits at the peak of this hierarchy.

Vect soared to power over his fractious people several millennia after the Fall. It is said he was merely a warrior-slave when Slaanesh tore its way into being. Once a low-born nothing sold to the pleasure cults for some abominable degradation, now he rules with both an iron fist and a hidden blade – one his detractors only realise is at their throats too late.

Despite Vect's self-asserted position of absolute power, Commorrite society is far from centralised. The Supreme Overlord reigns over a splintered civilisation of self-serving interests. These range from coordinated organisations to warring gangs that roam the fringes of society, and derelicts seeking survival at the Dark City's desolate outskirts. Commorragh remains an incomprehensibly vast webway hub, and within its environs are renegades, criminals and mercenaries from many cultures, not to mention the masses of captives from every corner of the galaxy. All of this writhes under the boot of Vect.

SPLINTERED POWER

The Lord of Darkness marshals the schemes of those below him like the composer of a great work, upholding the autonomy of the city's entities while keeping them at each other's throats. Vect both ensures that there are no threats to his power, and that the ruthless meritocracy of Commorragh strengthens those within it. Whatever one's station in the Dark City, there is always a blade waiting in the dark, or a sheen of poison on the lips of a lover.

Amongst the most powerful institutions of Commorragh are the Kabals, each a kind of militaristic cartel or private army, – such as Vect's own Kabal of the Black Heart. These gang-like societies maintain their power via the realspace raids their ruling Archons launch. The Wych Cults, meanwhile, stage incredible displays of gladiatorial debaucheries within immense arenas, feeding Commorrite society with gory spectacles. In the bowels of the Dark City's pitch-black underworld, the Haemonculi Covens practice their arts of flesh sculpting, soul syphoning and vile regeneration, their costly services always in high demand. Surrounding these three pillars of Commorragh are mercenaries fulfilling subtler requirements. Through the striking of contracts between these factions, realspace raids often contain uneasy allies – such pacts evaporating once the spoils are divided.

COMMORRAGH'S KABALS

The Kabals of Commorragh resemble pirate bands, noble households and criminal cartels. Their numbers are made of sadists, slavers, torturers, murderers and thieves. Kabals are in a state of constant conflict, their webs of alliances and rivalries ever-shifting in Commorragh's brutally meritocratic and labyrinthine political landscape.

The Kabals form Commorragh's primary military strength and the upper tiers of its hierarchy. It is from their realspace raids that the majority of slaves are procured. Even the smallest of the Kabals number hundreds of Drukhari, with territory spread over hideouts, safe houses and other hidden locations. The largest have millions in their ranks, control vast swathes of Commorragh and have galaxy-wide influence thanks to their endless stream of raids and rampant piracy.

ORDER FROM ANARCHY

In the murderous society of Commorragh, Drukhari with aspirations for enormous power – which is the overwhelming majority – will easily make enemies and draw unwanted attention. This makes them vulnerable, and makes reaching the heights they wish to achieve almost impossible. Thus, most Drukhari wish to join a Kabal, though competition is fierce and the initiation rites extremely bloody. Within a Kabal there is the safety of numbers and a ladder of hierarchy they can climb. An attack on a Warrior of a Kabalite is seen as an attack on them all, and so a modicum of order is maintained – Kabals will not make dangerous enemies unless they see their own position as being strong enough to withstand the potential fallout. This does not mean, however, that particular individuals in a rival Kabal cannot, or should not, be eliminated, it just means that the way in which they are removed has to be more subtle. So does this power structure incentivise murder by subterfuge and careful scheming.

Due to the continuous stream of fresh recruits, the large quantity of a Kabal's number that are outside Commorragh on raids and the networks of escape routes and secondary bases they employ, it is almost impossible to wipe out a Kabal in its entirety. Only Asdrubael Vect has the power and influence to carry out

such an action without triggering city-wide outrage or a cascade of successive skirmishes, as the webs of Kabal alliances declare war on each other in the aftermath. Nonetheless, Vect ensures that gang warfare remains rife throughout Commorragh, claiming the weak and raising the strong.

KABALS AT WAR

Carrying out raids is the most important task for Kabalites and Kabals. Not only do they yield great bounties of slaves and offer feasts of agony to delight in, there is also immense personal and political prestige to be gained in returning to Commorragh having successfully planned and carried out a raid. By impressing their fellow Commorrite citizens, a Kabal asserts dominance over its rivals.

Thus, the largest Kabals are always raiding. Some may have scores – or even hundreds – happening simultaneously, attacking world after hapless world and winning political as well as military victories.

In the same way that Kabalite Archons scheme to acquire power and outmanoeuvre their rivals, they plan their raids to meticulous detail. They torture existing slaves and employ scouts and mercenaries to acquire as much knowledge as possible of the world they intend to strike. They also pay the Haemonculi enormous sums for more esoteric means of surveillance, such as whisperglass mirrors, flocks of invisible familiars and parasitically invested abductees. Though costly, the rewards of a successful raid make the investment more than worth it.

In battle, the Kabalites seek every advantage they can over the enemy, viewing concepts such as honour or valour as weaknesses to be exploited. They strike where the enemy is most

vulnerable and retreat where they encounter organised resistance, striking hard and fast to cripple command and control systems and to spread confusion and terror. Ambush, hit and run tactics and trickery are as much a part of their arsenal as advanced weapons, and they use them to full effect.

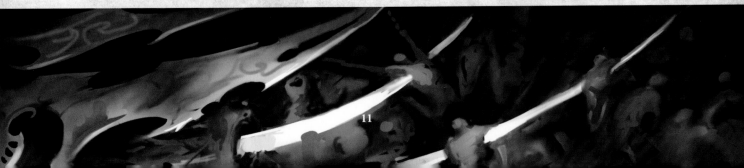

WYCH CULTS

The inherent poise, grace and athleticism of the Drukhari is raised to a high art in the numerous Wych Cults throughout Commorragh. In fearless displays of sublime craft, these gladiatorial institutions entertain the powerful and influential denizens of the Dark City with lurid spectacles, providing a feast of agonies for their hungry-eyed audiences.

The constant demand in Commorragh for extreme experiences, exotic suffering and passionate diversions – to stave off crushing ennui, catastrophic civil war and the gnawing void within the Drukhari's souls – is catered for, to an extent, by the arenas of the Wych Cults. Most Wych Cults maintain at least one arena, built into the lofty citadels and blade-edged ziggurats of their domains, in which nightly displays of violence are perpetrated with elegance and speed.

To compare even the least of these arenas to the greatest of Mankind's stadia is to compare a glittering palace to a mud hut. In some arenas, multi-level simulacra of alien cities, dense jungle or countless evocative dioramas ring to the sound of bloodshed. Wyches engage in battle with choice captives, monstrous beasts or even each other to the bloodthirsty roars of those citizens wealthy or manipulative enough to buy a seat. Some arenas are toroid in shape – encircling Commorragh's highest pinnacles –

and host lethally competitive death races of jetbike-riding Reavers. Other amphitheatres are laced with ingenious traps or accommodate anti-grav tournaments of swooping killers. Some arenas even drift through the Dark City, allowing galleries of crowds to follow skyboard-riding Beastmasters and their packs of frightening thrall creatures as they hunt down terrified prey through Commorragh's dark alleys.

The diverse warriors – known as Hekatarii – within the Wych Cults wield a wildly divergent array of exotic tools to maim, entrap, slash and skewer. Vicious hooks, weighted flails, barbed meshes and innumerable outlandish armaments requiring huge skill are employed to flaunt the user's finesse. They wear little in the way of armour; their defence is their speed and agility, displaying their arrogance as they dodge the clumsy blows of the foe. Any edge is grasped as they seek to outdo their rivals. The consumption of endless varieties of stimulants and combat drugs

result in bursts of speed, heightened sensorial clarity or stranger effects, depending on which cocktail is in vogue.

BEYOND THE ARENA

Wych Cults are thousands-strong societies of gladiatorial bloodletters. In addition to their arenas, they maintain vast training complexes, beast menageries and exotic armouries. Their terrifyingly graceful warriors typically revolve around a single, extremely deadly Succubus – a star of the arenas celebrated for her murderous skill. Beneath her are lesser Succubi that may lead Circles of several dozen Wyches. Almost every Wych Cult enjoys the patronage of a powerful Archon. This arrangement ensures the Cult rarely runs short of slaves or exotic elixirs, and that the Archon gains the usually reliable allegiance of exceptional blademasters for their raids. When a Wych Cult with a strong reputation stages its own realspace raid, other factions will pay handsomely for the privilege of fighting alongside them.

HAEMONCULUS COVENS

Commorragh is a place of nightmare, and nothing encapsulates its ancient evil and inventive malice quite like the Covens of the Haemonculi. These twisted fraternities of torturer-alchemists practice vile arts of life and death from their lairs in the Dark City's gnarled underworld. They are crucial to the Drukhari's continued survival, yet their grisly skills always comes at a price.

Haemonculi are wizened monsters, geniuses of insane and unnatural technologies and are universally feared by the rest of Commorragh. Though each pursues their own, dark avenues of unspeakable science, every Haemonculus is a master artisan who offers a wealth of unpleasant services to those who can afford them. They deal in body modification, the distillation of potions and elixirs, and the extraction of screams from their victims and patients alike.

Like-minded Haemonculi gather into Covens that maintain sprawling territories of cells, laboratories and chem-distilleries among far more esoteric industries. Cavern-like voids, fields of bubbling vats and byzantine chambers no other Drukhari would ever wish to visit form the realms of many Covens. Twisting corridors formed from still-living subjects – with dim lamps set into the occasional empty eye socket – lead to grim abattoirs and racks of viscera-spattered torment slabs. To cross these ancient fleshcrafters is not only to risk an extended stay in their oubliettes of pain, held down and carved apart by their personal retinues of surgically augmented Wracks. It is to risk the withholding of a Haemonculus' art when it is needed most, for they have the power over life and death.

DAMNATION ETERNAL

Though incredibly long-lived by Human standards, Aeldari are not immortal. To avoid death, and the hunger that waits to claim their soul beyond, most Drukhari enter into a pact with one or more Haemonculi. The client voluntarily relinquishes a piece of their flesh: a finger, a flap of skin or a whole limb. The original flesh is kept secure and fresh, and from it the Haemonculus can regenerate the patron's entire body. Even a corpse that has been all but destroyed can be restored to its former glory. Many Drukhari put such a bargain off as long as they dare, for a Coven's price

is a permanent portion of their client's soul. Nevertheless, as Drukhari risk a violent death in the Dark City every day, and as even the most arrogant recognise their prey are not without primitive weapons, the Haemonculi are never short of customers.

Drukhari raids strike hard and fast, seizing bounties of captives and venting their pain-lust upon those they kill before slipping back into the webway. They bear away their own wounded or killed and deliver them to the Haemonculi, who set to work assisted by semi-sentient Engines of Pain, such as the Talos. Provided the ghastly process is enacted swiftly enough, and the Drukhari's strong spirit still resonates in what remains of their flesh, their animus will slowly regenerate along with their physical form.

The key to this loathsome procedure, like so many aspects of Drukhari culture, is pain. The mortal remains of the Drukhari are sealed inside crystal-fronted pods, arrayed in feeding circles around the Haemonculus' torment slabs and torture racks. As the fleshcrafter peels apart suitable victims beneath, the semi-cocooned Drukhari within the caskets are saturated with the writhing captive's agony and screams, drinking in the suffering. If they absorb enough over such torturous sessions, their red-raw forms, grimacing and leering, form within the caskets as they consume every shred of fevered pain. Then their bones, sinews, gelatinous viscera, bloody flesh and, finally, pallid skin eventually regrow.

DARK EXPERIMENTERS

By granting this form of hideous immortality, the Haemonculus Covens grow immensely wealthy and powerful, capable of demanding the superior spoils of raids. Despite their private obsessions, Haemonculi relish the opportunity to

exhibit their talents in person, sometimes performing their own raids as grim experiments of their creations. With ghoulish curiosity they unleash Cells of their servile apprentice Wracks and packs of grossly swollen Grotesques, eager to test their masters' latest psychotorture devices or venomous concoctions.

KABAL OF THE BLACK HEART

VECT'S WILL MADE MANIFEST

The Kabal of the Black Heart is Asdrubael Vect's military arm and the enforcer of his will. It is the oldest and greatest Kabal of its kind, formed by Vect himself during his meteoric rise to power to become Supreme Overlord of the Dark City.

THE RISE OF VECT

For millennia after the Fall, there were but a handful of noble houses that dominated the Dark City of Commorragh. It was their exclusive realm, and they slaughtered with impunity any who threatened their domination. The entirety of the city was utterly stagnant, overflowing with corruption and elitism. When Asdrubael Vect rose, he changed everything.

Vect is rumoured to originate from Commorragh's slave caste. As a result, the nobility underestimated him time and time again as he ascended through Commorragh's ranks. In secret, his group – the Cult of the Black Heart – inserted agents into every noble household. As his influence grew, so did the size of his following. Careful to appear at all times removed from the deeds committed by his followers, and determined that no rival should have a negative claim against him, Vect never had blood on his hands. His agents carried out the necessary bladework, and laced the correct meals and beverages with poison to smooth their lord's ascension. Vect could not permit the noble houses to ally together against him. He renamed his followers the Kabal of the Black Heart, and they in turn named him Supreme Overlord.

Blinded by their own arrogance, most of Commorragh's nobility did not see what Vect was doing, the power that he was accruing, until they were helpless to stop it. Thus, those noble houses and other criminal groups that remained intact after Vect rose adopted the Kabal structure to survive.

VECT'S OWN KABAL

The Kabal of the Black Heart is sprawling organisation, so vast that it supports numerous rival Archons, all with their own factions, gangs and agendas. Whilst all vie for Vect's patronage, competition almost never results in murder, for the Supreme Overlord does not look kindly on those who damage, break or destroy his tools. In addition, these Archons – immensely powerful and fear-inducing individuals in their own right – only dare to challenge Vect in their remotest fantasies. Even this they indulge in with great risk, for it is rumoured that, to Vect, treachery is a stench that pours off those who pose a threat.

With millions upon millions of Drukhari in the Kabal, the sheer might of the Black Heart makes it ostensibly invincible. It would take an alliance of many of the greatest Kabals to even match their numbers of warriors, something that – due to Commorragh's merciless politics – is far from likely. Thanks to the incredible power of the Kabal, as well as the inherent status that comes from being the Supreme Overlord's personal army, the Black Heart is able to operate more as a unified whole than can any institution in Commorragh. Vect's lesser Archons inspire the kind of apparent widespread loyalty no other Overlord can count on. If this military might was not great enough for the Kabal to assert total dominance over all of Commorragh, it has also formed a pact with the Cult of Strife, further strengthening Vect's position.

The Kabal of the Black Heart employs an army of spies and agents to serve at Vect's behest – its informers dwelling within every stratum of Commorrite society. Archons claiming to be acting independently have formed agreements with competing Haemonculi to provide the Kabal with information that can be compared and correlated for veracity. From the secrets of excruciated prisoners, to details of the pacts different covens have made and even knowledge of the latest works, there are some ancient Haemonculi who privately worry Vect's minions seek to render their arcane brotherhoods irrelevant.

The Black Heart has even secreted agents into the wider Aeldari race – aboard craftworlds of the Asuryani, amongst the Ynnari and on Exodite worlds – and some have successfully infiltrated Harlequin masques. Thus, Vect and his Kabalites are always multiple steps ahead of their rivals, and no action against the Black Heart is too small for him to take notice. The Supreme Overlord underestimates no-one, and knows a threat can come from any corner. This colossal spy network also means that any raids carried out in Vect's name by his Archons are done under his scrutiny. Every Archon knows their actions are being judged, and that the Supreme Overlord will have devised contingency plans for every eventuality. On the other hand, should they fail in any way, they will undoubtedly incur his wrath. Knowing that Vect could be displeased is a very powerful motivator for the Archons of the Black Heart. As a result, they carry out their devastating raids with lethal precision and bring back vast numbers of slaves to appease the Supreme Overlord.

Mistrusted allies and hated rivals all flocked to the Great Wake – that most ostentatious of events that marked the supposed death of Asdrubael Vect. It was, of course, the Supreme Overlord himself who had the last laugh, at the eternal expense of so many of his guests.

THE ETERNAL CYCLE

Asdrubael Vect is what is known in Drukhari society as 'half-born'. Due to the Aeldari race's long gestation period, artificially grown Drukhari are far more commonplace. This process is done by implanting a fertilised egg into one of the amniotic tubes that honeycomb the breeding-walls of the Haemonculi's lairs. Using a repulsive, insectile science developed many millennia ago, the embryo's growth can be hyperaccelerated within these tubes, each newly grown specimen wriggling from its chrysalis-sac in a drizzle of fluids before being taken away by Wrack attendants. These 'half-born' are viewed with contempt by the rarer Trueborn Drukhari, who believe them to be inherently inferior.

KABALS UNCOUNTED

Every one of Commorragh's numerous Kabals is different, waging war and conducting devastating raids the manner it deems most effective. These methods are often extensions of how a given Kabal initially rose to prominence, be it through savage gangland battles, a shared proclivity for gruesome aesthetics or the conceit of its single-minded Archon.

KABAL OF THE FLAYED SKULL

Besides the Kabal of the Black Heart, no force in Commorragh boasts as much military power as the Kabal of the Flayed Skull. Its Overlord is Vraesque Malidrach, a savage warrior who earned fame for his own unique brand of high-speed violence as a low-born Reaver. This was a formative experience for him, and even now he slaughters his foes in swift, shocking raids. The Kabal's base of operations is the Poisoned Crown, one of the highest and most jagged peaks in all of Commorragh. Encrusted on its vast flanks are innumerable docks and grav-moorings, and around them is an ever-shifting cloud of Voidraven Bombers and Razorwing Jetfighters. Overlord Malidrach is a renowned master of airborne warfare, gladly adopting new strategies being developed in Commorragh's arenas should they be spectacular and violent enough. Such is his renown that Hellions and Reavers flock to his banner, desperate to fight alongside him, and a great many Scourges have sold their loyalty to him also.

KABAL OF THE POISONED TONGUE

Few of the Kabals are as insidious as that of the Poisoned Tongue. Its agents are insinuated throughout Commorragh's necrotic veins. A vastly powerful organisation, it has earned its niche through the shameless misleading and wrong-footing of its rivals. The Kabal's members will gladly orchestrate failures and 'accidents' to enact an elaborate scheme of framing and scapegoating, to ensure certain rivals and 'allies' receive the blame. Before launching their own realspace raids, the Kabal's warriors make great use of infiltration tactics, assassinations and massed poisoning to weaken the foe prior to battle. They also plant false information, ensuring that wherever they strike the foe is least prepared to meet their onslaught.

Lady Aurelia Malys leads the Kabal, an intellectual titan whose ability to predict her enemies' manoeuvres borders on the supernatural. She has been at the heart of many of the Dark City's most deadly intrigues, and safely steered her Kabal through the greatest of treacheries. When Vect was 'murdered', his jubilant enemies gathered in a Great Wake to gloat, but Malys saw through the ploy and disappeared into the webway with her Kabal, thereby avoiding Vect's vengeful massacre.

KABAL OF THE OBSIDIAN ROSE

Even the lowliest Drukhari of the Kabal of the Obsidian Rose is clad in the most exquisitely crafted armour and finely honed weaponry. The Kabal controls the greatest swathe of weapons shops in the Dark City. Thanks to its Overlord, Aestra Khromys, it maintains an iron grip on Commorragh's arms trade. Such is the quality of the arms and armour it produces, just one item would be a prized instrument to a minor Kabal. To Khromys, perfection is the benchmark against which all the artefacts created in her workshops must be measured, and this exacting standard is applied to every area of life for all her Kabalites. Before a raid, the Kabal's warriors go through intensive training, practising physical steps and shots, and contingency planning to perfection. This they do to display what they see as their inherent superiority, over both the foe and rival Kabals. Those Kabalites who fail to meet Khromys' precise standards frequently find themselves setting an example for all – impaled on the Kabal's vehicles' bladed vanes, alongside captives.

KABAL OF THE LAST HATRED

The Drukhari of the Kabal of the Last Hatred are obsessed with forbidden arts. Many observers speculate about their motives, wondering whether they wish to transcend mortality entirely or destroy the Aeldari race, enslaving whatever entity is born from the remains. Regardless of the truth, their ambition is undeniable, and they will carry out any depraved act to see it realised – they prosecute their kin-strife against Asuryani, Exodites and especially the Ynnari with incredible viciousness. The Kabal is famous for its pain-farms and its incredible talent for keeping captives alive far longer than should be possible. Its members strap the still-living bodies of victims to their raiding craft in battle, and such is their expertise that they are able to prevent a soul from leaving a cadaver when it would usually depart.

KABAL OF THE DYING SUN

With proportionally more Trueborn in its number than any other, the Kabal of the Dying Sun is of truly ancient origin. Drukhari of overweening pride, they disdain anything that is not millennia old and even view Vect himself as a

OTHER KABALS

The diversity of warfighting methods among the various Kabals is limitless. Though some Kabals are particularly powerful, with enormous influence, many more circle the peripheries of Commorrite politics, planning their ascension to dominance. The Kabal of the Severed goes to war with numerous attack craft, to strike with speed and precision. Others prefer massive firepower, such as the Kabal of the Storm's Spire and the Kabal of the Bloody Scream, which purchase or produce numerous Ravagers and employ considerable numbers of Scourges. In contrast, others relish nothing more than the splash of their foes' blood on their face in the heat of close combat. Kabals including the Shuddering Blade and the Silver Fang love these bloodbaths, where they can hear the rattle of their enemies' last breaths and bathe in their screams of pain. Others make unusual alliances a part of their scheming – members of the Kabal of the All-Seeing Eye are highly secretive, acting as influential power brokers who have formed working relationships with highly skilled Haemonculi, while the Kabal of the Fiend Ascendant works closely with Wych Cults and Harlequins. Some are stranger still. The Drukhari of the Kabal of the Thirteenth Whisper shroud their faces during their nightmarish raids, and are believed to have formed alliances with Mandrakes. When the Kabal attacks, tides of shadow proceed it, whilst horrors stalk the surrounding darkness.

usurper. Preferring to raid at sunset, they strike out from their stronghold called the Pinnacle of Disdain, a nigh on impenetrable mountain. Their Overlord, Vorl-Xoelanth, is obsessed with turning light and hope to darkness and despair. What few – if any – outside the Kabal know, is that the Drukhari of the Dying Son possess ancient fragments of forbidden arcana from the old Aeldari Empire, though the members themselves poorly understand these psychically charged artefacts. With the power to snuff out suns, exterminate sentient races and suck the life force from worlds, the Kabal uses them only as a last resort. Anything could go wrong, and such an act would inevitably draw much unwanted attention.

THE LORDS OF THE IRON THORN

Rulers of the sub-realm of Pandaimon, the Lords of the Iron Thorn possess one of the mightiest fleets of Raiders and Ravagers of any of the Commorrite Kabals, and they supply the Kabal of the Black Heart itself with these sleek weapons of war. Their symbol, etched on the smooth flank of a raiding vehicle, is a great mark of quality. This is a reputation the Archons of the Kabal have worked long and hard to achieve, following a failed rebellion by a past master against Asdrubael Vect. Now, their grav-docks and weapon shops – constantly ringing with the clangour of slave-driven industry – are so sprawling, they could cover the surface of a small moon. Such is the vast number of slaves the Kabal's

forges require, its Kabalites are incredibly active raiders. They believe strongly in the application of overwhelming firepower and the supremacy of their craft when defeating the crude engines of the lesser races.

KABAL OF THE BROKEN SIGIL

The Drukhari of the Broken Sigil take enormous pleasure in inducing utter terror in their foes, striking at the most idyllic, ordered and prosperous worlds to bring about confusion and despair. So strong is their love of inflicting fear upon their foes that many rivals look down upon the Broken Sigil's Overlord Xerathis, for how predictable he is to both them and the enemy. Xerathis takes great delight in repeatedly unleashing bombardments of hallucinogenic gas on his foes, or hijacking their communications. The Overlord and his Kabalites state that any price they pay for forewarning the enemy is made more than worth it for the feast of terror they can gorge upon when battle is joined. One such price is their notoriety among the worlds of the Imperium, and particularly among the Deathwatch and the Ordo Xenos of the Inquisition – both of which have targeted Xerathis directly, though he shows little concern over this kind of attention. Instead, he boasts what fine slaves post-Human warriors make.

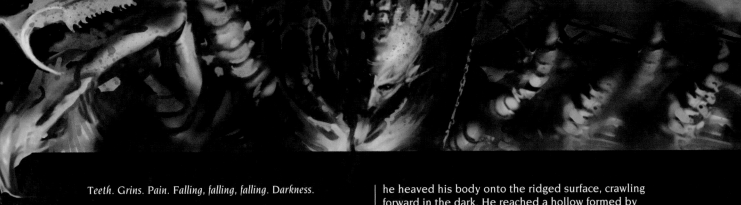

Teeth. Grins. Pain. Falling, falling, falling. Darkness.

Colour Sergeant Pranda awoke with a scream. An unformed nightmare still coiled in his memory. He screamed again when he realised he could see nothing before his open eyes, and again when the pain hit him.

A stabbing agony shot through his shoulder and across his chest. After a wave of nausea, he realised he was on his back somehow. Pranda's legs were twisted up against some obstacle, his head and shoulders likewise. It took several attempts to move his bruised right arm to feel around him, while he couldn't move or even feel his left. Behind his crooked neck, Pranda touched some hard surface and – groping blindly – sensed a draught move around him, over him, under him… under? He reached down and felt nothing, an emptiness through which a damp wind blew.

Falling.

The splinter of memory jabbed into his subconscious. Pranda had been falling.

Teeth. Grins. Pain.

'Emperor, help me!' he whispered, memory flooding back as feeling grew in his compressed legs.

He'd been taken on Coriola. Taken with, with… Throne, half the regiment! The sky had darkened and they'd come like flying horrors from childhood fables. They'd stalked from places that should have been secure, stabbing and slashing. Pranda had been in the third line, holding the company standard. Barbed chains that bit through his flak jacket had wrapped around his left arm and been pulled taught, dislocating it violently.

With gasps and stifled yelps, Pranda awkwardly inched his way upwards, bracing himself between shoulder and legs. There was a rime of mere gloom above him, delineated against the utter blackness around him. He reached what his painful back told him was the sharp lip of a horizontal surface. Pranda managed to grip a ridge before a sense of helplessness swept over him, magnifying his fear. When a hiss and rustle swept up from the dark depths, Pranda pushed away with his legs and flung his right arm over the edge. Adrenaline surged through his tiring limbs, tears covering his face. Something came loose under his scrabbling boots and he heard a screech below. Pranda hardly breathed as

he heaved his body onto the ridged surface, crawling forward in the dark. He reached a hollow formed by angular buttresses and cowered, straining his ears for any noises of pursuit as his eyes panned over a hellish landscape.

In shades of grey, bruise purple, dirty cyan and vague hues he couldn't name, a forest of dark spires and jutting spurs stretched as far as Pranda could see. To a city rat like him, it was like a thousand hive cities crammed together and somehow bent out of true. Blood-red lights winked in the depths and ghostly orbs hung far above him, highlighting every sharp edge in a wan illumination. He retched drily as the twisted perspective of oddly angled buildings disoriented him. Distant detonations and bestial cries echoed strangely, and there was a chemical stink to the air. It was like a battlefield at war's end, he thought, when the smell of blood, effluent, promethium and cordite all meshed.

Pranda turned, his gaze drawn by sleek shadows swimming across what – for sanity's sake – he called the sky. Now his eyes were growing accustomed to the ever-present darkness, he saw one narrow shape emerge into the pale 'starlight'. Its sweeping curves and beaked prow moved through the gloom like an oceanic predator. With a jolt of recognition, he remembered being aboard such a craft, but could only recall fractured glimpses, sounds or feelings – the screams of men and women of his regiment alongside the simultaneously sibilant and rasping speech of their captors. He recollected eating and drinking something vile and shuddered at the thought.

Then they threw us overboard. Holy Emperor, they kicked us off like we were already dead weight. Throne knows how far I fell.

Pranda reached into the webbing at his waist for his personal icon, carved from a shard of shrapnel two campaigns since. If anyone was responsible for his survival, it was the God-Emperor, he knew – but the icon wasn't there. Instead he pulled out what looked like a short knife that wasn't his. The handle was wound with greasy ribbing, through which poked sharp spikes. Maybe he'd grabbed it from one of the xenos before he'd been pushed into empty space, he thought. He heaved in a breath, his mind clearing with the fresh pain from the needle-like hilt of the dagger.

Gripping the blade and gritting his teeth against its bite into his palm, he crawled slowly out of his hollow, then

set off at a run. A shout went up to his left, followed by laughter and swift footsteps. Pranda ran at a crouch, cradling his useless left arm. He squeezed under a balustrade and half-slid down a steep incline, recalling gang hunts from his youth where they would chase down some unlucky interloper. Pranda knew there was no hope in standing his ground, no permanent refuge. The only chance of living was to keep moving, even if he hadn't a clue where he was going.

He stopped. He breathed. He listened. Then Pranda ran again. Sloping alleyways twisted and forked. Dark portals yawned at every turn and the insufficient light shifted in colour and intensity, wrecking his sense of direction and sending his heart racing with every half-glimpsed threat.

This place is a maze!

Now he could hear movement to his right and behind him. Pranda breathed hard, the weariness of before swept aside, and even the pain in his arm and chest felt dulled. Skidding around a corner, he caught sight of running shapes that flashed through slivers of dim light. They darted towards a vast expanse spread out before him. It was some kind of plaza carved out between the monumental buildings, studded with man-high protrusions like the teeth of a micadragon. Pranda backed into the lee of a masked statue to avoid the hunters' gaze. It was deformed and hideous. One of its three pale hands bore a ritualised blade similar to the one he still held. Pranda's own hand was now slowly dripping with blood from the multiple small wounds inflicted by the blade's barbs.

Suddenly, three soldiers broke cover, dodging and stumbling between the tooth-like obelisks. Guardsmen! The light glinted on the unmistakable chrome helmet one still retained. She was helping her comrade, whose leg seemed broken, while a bare-armed bruiser guarded their rear, glancing about with obvious paranoia. It was warranted. Pranda could see flashes of pale skin and glinting weapons weave their way towards the trio, making the Humans seem pitifully slow and awkward.

They're not going to make it! Run, for Throne's sake, run!

Two graceful Drukhari, clad in tight-fitting bodygloves, leapt at the rearguard from separate sides. The soldier spat a curse and shouted at his cohorts to run. A lash

caught his arm, pulling him off balance before a wicked dagger sliced a length of skin from his arm. It flapped, still attached, as he flailed and screamed. Precise flicks of the Drukhari's' curved knives severed the tendons behind his knees as the hunters danced around him, effortlessly avoiding his thrashing sweeps.

The soldier with the broken leg stumbled onto his front, then yelled in shock, pushing himself away from the ground. Beneath him, Pranda saw the man's shadow bulge and then reach up, two arms grabbing his neck. The Guardsman struggled, weeping and screaming until he was pulled bodily into wherever the arms originated. A puff of vapour like chilled air was all that marked his disappearance. His helper, open-mouthed with terror, backed away. She suddenly broke into a run, away from her bloody comrade, but only managed three strides before something struck her shoulder and she was yanked into the air. Three Drukhari on anti-grav devices circled each other, one holding the claw-tipped wire clasping the Guardsman. She swung between them while each darted in for a cruel strike, cutting away chunks of flesh that rained down as she rose higher and her screams vanished.

No, no, no!

Pranda's limbs shook, his muscles cramped in fear and his skin crawled. He crouched, trembling, unable to unsee the horrific ends of his fellow Guardsmen. It was when the fear reached its peak that the three-armed statue bent slowly down to wrap a wiry hand around his neck. He couldn't move. He couldn't tear his eyes away from the faceless, metal mask of the thing that held him. The pale, dusty and skinless flesh he'd taken for stone flexed as the thing brought up a small device in front of its mask. He barely heard the whisper of the xenos' own voice, but a chilling perfection of High Gothic was emitted by the device as the creature addressed him.

'Your gifts to the port are usually worthless detritus, already dead or too senseless to be of use, but my master knows surprises can happen. I'm sure you like surprises, little thing, don't you?'

The skinned xenos easily prized the barbed dagger from Pranda's grasp, careful to avoid the stimulant injectors in the handle. Colour Sergeant Pranda managed a desperate, silent plea to the Emperor, but it would not be his last.

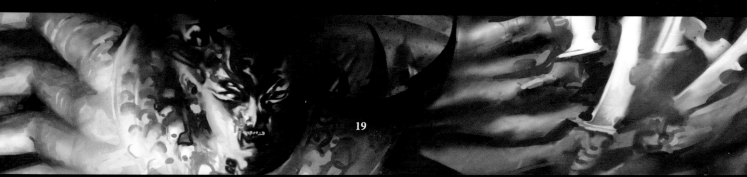

CULT OF STRIFE

EXCELLENCE EMBODIED

The Wych Cult of Strife is the largest and most influential of its kind, far outstripping the countless other murder-cliques in Commorragh. Its devoted spectacle-addicts attribute the Cult's still swelling power to its star Succubus – Lelith Hesperax, the Queen of Knives – while she ensures the thousands of Wyches at her call maintain their deadly superiority over their rivals.

Masters of the savagely violent opening act that grips the jaded interest of even its most long-standing detractors, the Cult of Strife is envied and despised across Commorragh for its peerless and agonisingly beauteous performances. The circles of the Cult of Strife are each led by a lesser Succubus, ever watchful of the poise and grace of their mistress, Her Excellence, Lelith Hesperax. Her nigh on supernatural combat skills, incredible sense of occasion and ability to mould her audience's wild emotions with teases and raptures of agony, make Lelith a subject of devotion and ambition. With such a sublime exemplar of the Wych Cults' diverse arts at their head, the Hekatarii of the Cult strive to push themselves to achieve the perfection Lady Hesperax embodies. Lelith cares not that they do so for purely selfish reasons – namely their

own advancement. She makes quick and brutal examples of any of the Cult who displease her.

The Cult of Strife benefits from an unusually strong bond with the Kabal of the Black Heart – the dangerous cartel of Asdrubael Vect himself. It is rumoured the Supreme Overlord even attends the rare spectacles when Lelith herself takes to the arena, though into the den of such exquisite murderers he surely only sends a holo-surrogate or vat-cloned proxy. This known compact ensures that few of the Cult of Strife's rivals would ever make a blatant move against it, and means that the Kabalites of Commorragh's master are often joined by the Cult's ferocious warriors during their raids into realspace. The mutual benefits of Vect's all-powerful patronage and the reflected glory of Lelith's fame

ensure that the Cult's nightly, decadent arena extravaganzas are well attended. Many of Commorragh's privileged elite will pay extortionate fees in rare captives or subtle exotica, cede portions of their territory or undertake lethal errands for a few precious moments among the black-veined living jade of the Crucibael's galleries.

The Crucibael is the Cult of Strife's primary arena, and the sovereign territory of the Queen of Knives. It is the most lavishly appointed and spectacular in all of Commorragh, with a capacity of well over a million. Just like Lelith's, its name is known far beyond the phantasmal boundaries of the Dark City. It has played host to countless legendary figures, and even the Phoenix Lord Jain Zar has graced its bloody sands with her consummate bladework. Combining its

LELITH HESPERAX

There has never been a fighter so sublime, of such cruel artistry and pallid beauty as Lelith Hesperax – so say the vicious and sadistic audiences privileged to witness her acts of inventive lethality. She is the undisputed mistress of the Drukhari's gladiatorial arenas and the greatest of the Succubi. Her skills in the arts of combat bear the mark of true genius and several lifetimes' worth of training. The purr of her voice is like honeyed velvet, though she rarely speaks, and while she remains aloof from the murderous politics of her people, Lelith is not unaffected by them. Her influential contacts, and her reputation as a giver of exquisite vitality through the spectacles she orchestrates, make her a subject of awe, fear and envy throughout the Wych Cults. Alone amongst them, Lelith declines the use of combat drugs. She sees them as a crutch for the weak, for they dull the visceral thrill of inflicting the killing blow and watching the lifeblood flow from her victims after a dozen crippling injuries. She is an expert in each of the exotic weapons wielded by the warriors of her Cult of Strife, yet Lelith herself is most frequently seen with a pair of knives. Such is her skill that these simple weapons are deadly to any creature. She strikes swifter than a snake, gifting parting caresses with flicks of the barbs in her hair.

roles as twisted circus and gluttonous feast hall, the Crucibael presents programmes of intense, emotive variety for the crowds to drink in. Through the expansive laser-grid of its toroid arena, gangs of Reavers hurtle at dangerous speeds. The bladevanes of their dart-like jetbikes tear open nearby rivals, while grav-talons smash those they overshoot into the arena's spine-lined walls. Liars and cheaters all, every advantage is taken to inflict stunning and improbable kills that threaten their own lives as much as their opponents'.

The wealth and power that flows into the Crucibael enables the Cult of Strife to entreat of master armourers and Haemonculi the finest or most unconventional weapons and stimulants they can provide. Razorflails are wielded as a twin pair of blades that – at first glance – resemble long, segmented swords, yet with a single flick of the wrist each splits apart to lash like a metallic whip. Hydra gauntlets, meanwhile, are made from a semi-sentient, extraplanar crystal, which a strong-willed wearer can compel to grow in a profusion of lethal edges, slicing apart anyone they can reach. Addictive compounds such as grave lotus, painbringer and splintermind

– while drastically shortening the user's life expectancy – are widely used to heighten combat performance or to savour a victim's anguish on higher planes of sensitivity.

The revenue from Lelith's blood games is also channelled into immense training academies that ruthlessly winnow out the weak, and into funding the Cult's own realspace raids. By sending her circles of Wyches, Reavers, Beastmasters and supporting gangs of Hellions to as many different prey worlds as possible, and by driving them – on pain of a horrific fate – to master every form of sublime killing, the Queen of Knives safeguards her Cult's hard-won credibility within Commorrite society. There truly is no method of death beyond the Cult of Strife's grasp.

Lelith has little patience for the complex counter-schemes and cunning webs of betrayals practised by the lords and ladies of the Kabals. Yet despite the supposedly cast-iron bond with Vect's Kabal of the Black Heart, her keen intellect has been put to use establishing multiple practical redundancies should his patronage ever wane. This possibility has lingered in the dark recesses of Lelith's mind more of late. It was in her own Crucibael

that Yvraine, the Daughter of Shades, was reborn as the Emissary of Ynnead, the Aeldari God of the Dead. Yvraine's violent apotheosis – after being bested by Lelith – unleashed not only scores of alien combatants upon Lelith's spectators, but also led to the latest of Commorragh's dysjunctions – severe ruptures in the Dark City's layered sub-realms that result in daemonic incursions.

In the wake of Yvraine's escape from Commorragh – and a rallying of support to awaken her whispering deity – Lelith has despatched numerous forces of skilled arena fighters to take up arms alongside Yvraine's disciples, the Ynnari. Some see this as the end of her long-standing protection by Vect, for the Supreme Overlord is thought to view the Ynnari with cold contempt. While Lelith's rivals probe the alliance for weaknesses, others wonder whether her apparent support for the Ynnari is all it seems. Is she truly endorsing what she sees as a way to defeat She Who Thirsts once and for all, as the Ynnari claim? Is she seeking a self-centred route to immortality without the cost of the soul debt? Or could it simply be that she seeks another confrontation with Yvraine, to test herself against the divine power of a god?

CULTS OF THE HEKATARII

Though in some ways the other Wych Cults of Commorragh have been overshadowed by the Cult of Strife, they have each carved out strongholds and territories, not to mention distinctive specialities. These niche fortes allow the rival Cults to draw their own crowds of appreciative epicureans, seeking unusual displays of violence, exquisite bloodfests or symphonies of pain.

Commorragh's population is far greater than even the Drukhari's puritanical kin aboard the craftworlds might guess. To cater to even a fraction of its pain-hungry deviants, Vect encourages the existence and rivalry of a great many Wych Cults. Amongst the sprawl of the Dark City's tenebrous realms, districts and subdimensions, the soaring towers of High Commorragh and the unwholesome disarray of its Underworld, there are many gladiatorial factions and sub-factions. Each seeks to supplant its rivals, take over their territories, prove mastery over every form of combat ever devised, and to do all of this to the baying of hundreds of thousands of paying spectators.

THE CURSED BLADE

Steeped in the treachery and deceit of the Dark City, the Cult of the Cursed Blade sees the betrayal of trust as the highest art form. Archons who seek alliances with the gladiators of the Nhexus Arena are seen as either trying to prove they can outwit the Cursed Blade, or as giving in to some deranged suicidal mania. The Cult's Wyches – and their ever strategising Succubi – are experts in wrong-footing their allies and their enemies both. Hidden blades and multifunctional weapons such as razorflails are favoured, as are poisoned barbs secreted under pallid skin and flick-blades implanted beneath exquisitely manicured nails.

By a perverted process of hyperaccelerated natural selection, the Cult of the Cursed Blade ensures only the strongest and most cunning within their ranks survive. This strength is employed with deep-seated guile and infinite adaptability. In the Nhexus Arena, famed for its myriad of lethal surprises – sometimes even set amid the audience galleries – a favoured performance of the Cult is to feign an alliance with an unwitting alien pawn. The combatant is given the hope that they may survive with the aid of the blisteringly fast warrior at their side, only to be turned on by their false friend. The warriors of the Cursed Blade savour the looks of shock and betrayal on their victims' faces as a delightful sweetmeat.

The Cult's treachery is scaled up to entire raids, sometimes planned to coincide with assaults by other invaders. Appearing without warning, they have helped defend Imperial worlds, T'au habitats and Asuryani craftworlds from ravening daemon hordes, brutal Ork butchers or myriad other galactic threats. Each time, the Cursed Blade instil a glimmer of hope in the defenders, before snuffing out such thoughts of salvation with their own brand of merciless cruelty.

THE RED GRIEF

The tight fitting wychsuits worn by all Hekatarii offer little physical protection. Instead, the Cults teach that the best defence is simply not to be there when the blade falls. The Cult of the Red Grief takes this obsession to the extreme. Its members push their lithe bodies and their preternatural reactions to reach velocities attained by few others.

Surging into the fray upon speeding Raiders, Venoms, jetbikes and skyboards, the Red Grief offers merely bloody blurs as targets, some of its raiding craft even releasing contrails of vaporous vitae from underslung racks of living bodies. Deigning to touch the ground only when right on top of their enemies, many coteries of the Cult's Wyches leap from their baroque barges as they swoop at full speed.

The Red Grief's lightning-fast aerial expertise over the hunting grounds of realspace is reflected in the visceral thrills offered by its arena. The Pit is built into the peak of a towering spire. Its translucent crystal galleries position its audiences on the edge of a dizzying plunge to their death far below, for they overlook a yawning gulf. Among the arena's struts and spars, Hellions and Reavers duel at breakneck speeds. Some unspool lengths of monofilament razor wire in their wake, so woe betide any opponent who doesn't carefully monitor their zigzagging manoeuvres. If struck at the speeds members of the Red Grief often fight at, these invisible meshes fillet the unwary into bloody fragments.

THE SEVENTH WOE

In the ancient myths of the Aeldari, the 'Seventh Woe' refers to the destruction of the maiden-god Lileath's hearth-moon at the hands of Kaela Mensha Khaine – a legend resonant with the loss of innocence. Ruled over by a competing triumvirate of Succubi, members of the Cult of the Seventh Woe are mutilators and enders of purity and virtue. Just as its rulers teach those born into their ranks to wield a blade before they can talk, so the Cult sees itself as a teacher to the entire galaxy, of the despair that lies at the heart of all existence.

This philosophy is enacted upon the battlefield through techniques designed to maim, rather than kill. Their shots and blows are aimed to sever tendons and shatter joints. In an echo of duels within their arena – in which the first to inflict thirteen shallow cuts is victorious – warriors of the Seventh Woe cripple the enemy with numerous lesser injuries. In their wake, they leave a carpet of mutilated bodies that write, in agony and in a creeping realisation, of greater torments to come. Once their opponents have been mangled and disabled, the Wyches of the Seventh Woe stalk amongst the screaming masses, inflicting slow tortures and unspeakable cruelties at their leisure.

THE BLADE DENIED

With sudden and violent improvisation, overcoming the greatest of handicaps is the hallmark of the Cult of the Blade Denied. It is an elder Wych House that specialises in the art of using its foes' weapons against them, of turning its enemies' apparent strength into a weakness that seals their doom. A recurrent and popular exhibition of the Cult members' skills is an unarmed, sometimes bound gladiator at the seeming mercy of a myriad of armed captives. Slipping their bonds and stealing their opponents' blades, the Wych's performance builds into a messy finale, with their multiple assailants skewered upon their own weapons.

As in their Helix arena, the Blade Denied are famed for stacking the odds against themselves during their frequent realspace raids. Attacking dug-in strongholds or outnumbering hordes of massed armoured vehicles, they employ pinpoint haywire attacks to turn bunkers and tanks into immobile tombs, and phantasm grenades to heighten mob fears. With the foe trapped and panicking, warriors of the Blade Denied proceed to take their time and pick apart their prepared victims, often pilfering their foes' weapons to cut

them down. Stories of defenders taking their own lives out of terror are often accounts of the Cult of the Blade Denied's grim art.

THE WRATH UNBOUND

Capable of entering a ritual, meditative state of berserk fury known in the Aeldari tongue as *Khaélas Maenaid* – the killing trance – Wyches of the Cult of the Wrath Unbound become indiscriminate butchers, as dangerous to their allies as to the enemy. Led by the Succubus Hythnamene Veilblood, the Wyches and Beastmasters of this Cult practise long and gory rituals before each performance or battle, gradually letting their intellect slip away and their hungry instincts take over.

The Cult is widely famed in Commorragh for its Beastmasters and the diversity of savage creatures they drive before them. Sinking into states of half-crazed consciousness, the shamanistic despoilers are little better than the feral beasts they dominate, and are a favoured sight in realspace raids by the Cult's patron Archon – Xethis Khuravok of the Kabal of the Baleful Gaze.

The Wrath Unbound is known to have 'hosted' the depraved renegade blademaster, Lucius the Eternal, within their arena. This is much to the chagrin of Lelith Hesperax, who seeks to capture and duel the arrogant slaughterer herself. The Cult found the absolute euphoria of the Khaélas Maenaid, as their howls and snarls rang through their arena, a pleasing harmony with the screams emitted by the renegade's cursed armour.

SKYHUNTERS

Skyboards are single-pilot, anti-gravity devices that are highly prized as symbols of independence. Many blade-edged skyboards are personalised with trophies or glyphs, though most have changed hands several times – won in ritual knife-fights or claimed as bounty. They are sensitive to the slightest motion, allowing their riders to jink at incredible speeds while firing their splinter pods into the foe with the depression of a heel stud.

Customised skyboards are employed by Beastmasters – calibrated for high speed while leaving their rider free to ply the lash on their feral charges. Skyboards are more commonly seen ridden by gangs of unruly Hellions. Not strictly members of the Wych Cults, they are nevertheless often seen in the arenas and broker temporary compacts with Cults to participate in realspace raids. Many are young Drukhari living on their wits in the fringes of society, while awaiting the chance to be chosen as a Kabalite. Others may have chosen exile, such as the self-professed underworld kingpin, Baron Sathonyx. He has managed what most Archon would consider beneath them and secured the allegiance of many gangs of street scum Hellions.

WAR ZONE:
GABAN

Isolated at the eastern reaches of the Segmentum Solar, the system of Carelle Minor sat far below the galactic plane. The Adeptus Mechanicus had hoped that the forge moon of Gaban, in Carelle's asteroid-strewn depths, would escape the notice of enemies. When a raid orchestrated by the Kabal of the Twisted Mantle struck Gaban, its rulers learned they had nowhere to hide.

Following hermetic protocols, the priestly rulers of Gaban had little contact with their parent forge world. The forge moon's religious elite had strict orders to shun outside signals in order to protect their secret work. The Xanthite faction had established this fortified archive of biosupplication to ensure their holy work was well-defended. Servitor-manned orbital weapons arrays and fleets of system monitors peered into the blackness of the void, while cohorts of Skitarii and up-gunned Kataphron battle units hunkered in suspension, ready to defend their masters' sacred work with their divinely augmented lives. What took place at Gaban could only be pieced together later from fragmented pict-safes, and by sifting the soup-like remains of the fallen Tech-Priests' brain matter.

The first recorded incident was a deep space radiation pulse that knocked out three of the watch stations on Carelle's furthest fringes. Investigation, repair and realignment proceeded as prescribed along strictures set in place millennia ago. The pulse's origin was never found. Five orbital cycles passed before a garbled message leaked out of the warp – a freighter, the voice screamed, in desperate need for aid. Gaban's lords ignored the signal, as scriptoral doctrine demanded. Over the following three cycles, a mounting itinerary of strange phenomena plagued Gaban. A cohort of Skitarii were recalled after marching out into the forge moon's salt wastes, claiming to be following divine imperatives. Rising numbers of Tech-Priests requested ocular augmentation, complaining about faulty lenses and illogical ephemera marring their vision in the darkest depths of their gene-vaults and cryotheatres.

Each of these occurrences was orchestrated far in advance by the scheming Archon Vradzek of the Kabal of the Twisted Mantle. Having tested the Tech-Priests' responses to various stimuli, and split their stunted attentions to focus on as many minor threats as possible, Vradzek unleashed his forces. Contracted, bought, bribed and threatened, the Archon had pulled dozens of strings to forge his realspace raid. Though many of his 'allies' believed they followed their own agendas beyond his ken, Vradzek knew each of their ambitions and played them off against each other. Many had been worming their way into Gaban's defences and infrastructure for hours before the Archon's fleet tore reality open.

Gaban's atmosphere warped under a bow wave of empiric energies as a hidden webway portal disgorged Vradzek's ships, bypassing the forge moon's outer defences to appear directly overhead. Pinpoint shafts of coruscating darkness severed macro-couplings to artillery barbicans and detonated missiles inside their silos. The conclave of Magi Biologis and Genetors that ruled Gaban attempted to recall their defence monitors. Through squalls of dirge-like interference, some of the conclave's ships reported that they were engaging further incursions throughout the system, while others relayed that they were being fired on by other ships in their squadron. Many never responded at all. Sweeping viral codes released by the Archon's agents spread through inter-ship transmissions, obscuring identification protocols, enacting violent decompressions and issuing conflicting imperatives.

On Gaban's salt wastes, crawling, multi-legged shapes – Gaban's motile geothermic spindlerigs – made their way towards defensive positions. These titanic, drill-footed contraptions were pulled back to provide protection with their armoured bulks, to shield the forge moon's power generatoria. Swarms of the Kabal's anti-grav transports and flocks of Scourges fell upon them. Haywire discharges and dark lance strikes crippled Gaban's clanking machines. Some juddered to a halt, while others continued on interminable courses, skewering the generatoria with diamond-tipped, stilt limbs.

In the dark crevices beneath Gaban's temple forges, contingency power plants fell. They became cold and lifeless as Mandrakes pulled themselves from the shadows and slaughtered the attending Enginseers, before escaping with their promised prize – the partitioned brains of the overseeing Manipulus.

On the outskirts of Gaban's primary gene-vault, coteries of Wyches from the Cult of the Razored Eye countercharged a rushing wedge of Serberys Sulphurhounds. As the Cult's patron, Vradzek had gifted them the razor-edged killing field and trench lines set up by the Adeptus Mechanicus, on the threat-laden caveat that they allow nothing to escape.

The privileged Trueborn of the Twisted Mantle and Incubi from the Shrine of Bloody Tears forced their way into the gene-vault's outer sanctum. The remaining biological portions of the Skitarii defenders were easy prey to volleys of poisoned shards, and their blessed bionic augmentations parted like cheap tin before the rain of klaive strikes. Stepping from a personal webway portal – forcibly redirected by Drukhari science – Archon Vradzek took command. He drove his force like a dagger into the gene-vault's heart, while a dozen separate engagements tore apart the devout Skitarii and Servitors.

Twist-limbed and scar-riven Wracks poured into the breach made by Vradzek. Their hovering masters of the Grimgeist Coven sent packs of monstrous Grotesques into the winding maze of corridors and cryochambers, while they swiftly co-opted the gene-vault's cogitator banks and tracked down the specimens Vradzek had ceded to them.

Within two hours, Vradzek had the entire forge moon in his grasp. The Archon's spies had monitored the station for some time and knew there would be no help coming. Some of the records the Imperium were later able to collate suggested the Drukhari tarried for three days upon Gaban after it fell, taking their time over the thousands of captives and draining the vaults dry of every specimen. The only corpses the Adeptus Mechanicus recovered were unfeeling Servitors and the jelly-like cranial residue that once cushioned their rulers' brains.

THE PROPHETS OF FLESH

EXEMPLARS OF EXCRUCIATION

Like a bloated, black cyst buried within Commorragh's strata of physical, social and political tissue, the Prophets of Flesh is a Coven with a level of influence that rightly worries many of the most powerful Archons, its anchoring tendrils of infection spreading. This Coven now seems impossible to cut out of the Dark City without repercussions that few are willing to risk.

The Prophets of Flesh is led by the Sculptor of Torments himself, Urien Rakarth, and basks in the long-standing patronage of Asdrubael Vect – alongside a clutch of other powerful Overlords. The Coven maintains its seemingly unassailable position through the quality of its breadth of services, supplying Archons, Succubi, fallen nobles, criminal parvenus and anyone who can afford their price. Yet its power is also strengthened through ruthless recoupment of payment, and an infinitely creative menu of excruciating fines to apply to those who attempt to renege. Many of Commorragh's elite also hold inescapable treaties of resurrection with the Prophets of Flesh, and would never dare risk the Coven's ire.

The Prophets of Flesh is amongst the largest of its kind. Though outstripped by some of the Kabals in size, the Coven maintains hundreds of Haemonculi. Each one delves into the horrors of their craft in often solitary pursuits, while suckling at the hub of genius represented by Urien Rakarth, hunched like a spider at the Coven's centre of power.

Every Haemonculus surrounds itself with several cells, each comprising dozens of their favoured creations and the twisted servants and apprentices known in some circles as Haemacolytes, but far more often as Wracks – for the changes wrought upon them by their masters. Wracks assist the Haemonculi in the brutal subdual of experimental subjects, and in some of the dissection and flesh modification that their masters consider beneath their rarefied talents.

Considered the apogee of the Dark City's underspire hierarchy, the Coven receives more Wrack supplicants than any other. To be a Prophet of Flesh is to be fearfully respected, yet the road to such power is a painful one indeed.

Upon induction, each Wrack's limbs are extensively branded, tattooed or unpleasantly altered according to the whims of their depraved master. Should a Wrack please their lord with especially inventive acts of sadism, they are

URIEN RAKARTH

The wrinkled, unhealthy skin stretched taut across Urien Rakarth's spare frame hides an even fouler soul, one twisted and ripened over millennia of abhorrent practices. Rumour within the Dark City tells of this ancient Haemonculus existing since before the days of the Fall. Rakarth has died and risen countless times, so often in fact that he savours death like a fine wine, and though he no longer returns to beauteous perfection, his toughened flesh heals at a ferocious rate. Rakarth's processes are a carefully concealed secret, but his skill and discretion in the arts of resurrection are beyond question, and his abilities are routinely courted by the most powerful in Commorragh. He is a master fleshcrafter, gene-splicer and a brewer of the most exquisite poisons. His hunch-backed, multi-limbed form is pumped full of the vilest toxins, and he wields dreadful tools with scalpel precision in a potent display of his expertise. Compound spines sprout from Rakarth's back, a leering face – selected from an extensive collection – is pinned to his skull and half-formed limbs poke from a fleshy mass, swaying with semi-sentient purpose. Some rivals think these are corruptions that have crept into his cycles of regrowth, yet in truth, they may merely be insane self-experiments by a mind so jaded that little piques its interest.

honoured with the removal of part of a marred limb, to be replaced with one of the countless unblemished body parts from the Prophets' flesh-libraries.

Each Prophet presides over thousands of Wracks and prefects of pain known as Acothysts. Their numbers allow the Coven to operate dozens of laboratories and abattoir-like surgeries, each stretching and spiralling for untold pitch-black miles through the transdimensional warrens beneath Commorragh's core. They extend into entire sub-realms that answer to none but Rakarth and his inner circle. Among some of these fleshworks and biofoundries, the Prophets' adepts dabble in hormone enrichment, muscle stimulation and hyperactive bone growth. The Haemonculi take a perverse pleasure in distorting the flesh, especially of those Drukhari who have crossed them. The Prophets' swollen creations include lobotomised Grotesques employed for extreme physical violence, and the part-mechanical and part-organic Engines of Pain – such as the Talos and Cronos.

Many members of the Prophets of Flesh dabble in soothsaying, despite the prohibition on psychic activity that pervades Commorragh. Seeking to learn truths of the universe by interpreting the effects of the atrocities they wreak, they are precise and diligent in their studies. With the detachment that truly superior beings show to lesser orders of life, they divine how the trauma of one conflict forms a psycho-temporal scar throughout an entire war zone, presaging ever more violent cruelties to come.

Competition for Rakarth's presence during a realspace raid, or to be granted the privilege of accompanying one of the Prophets' own carnivals of pain, swiftly turns lethal. Even minor raids by the Coven can sweep defences across entire planets. Flotillas of anti-grav transports carry the Prophets' latest monstrous creations in barbed cages, while cells of Wracks and throbbing menageries of Engines of Pain rush from hidden portals. Caravans of gigantic stellar barges swallow every stolen bounty until the world is left a blood-spattered

but silent orb. To view such ghoulish slaughter is one of the Dark City's finest tonics.

Rakarth feels little but faint amusement at such clamouring for his attention, satisfied that it masks any purpose deeper to his raids than merely lining his larder. Of late, the ancient creature has directed his Coven to the recovery of the Imperium's latest genetic dabblings, and he is on the verge of completing his collection of living Primaris subjects from every Space Marine Chapter. Rakarth seeks to study not Archmagos Cawl's insipid endeavours, but the far more interesting variety of mutations that have occurred as each of the Emperor's original efforts have degraded in varying ways throughout the millennia. Members of the Prophets of Flesh are also collecting on every favour – both in Commorragh and among their contacts in the Harlequins – to discover the location of Yvraine and her Ynnari disciples. Whether this is purely at Vect's behest, or to seize some insight only the God of the Dead can provide, remains to be seen.

THE CANVAS GALACTIC

Each Coven of Haemonculi is a schismatic brood of flesh-artisans. They are isolated creatures with their own private paranoias and compulsions, and while some do pass on elements of their lore, few share the full fruits of their vile craft. In the Dark City, however, there is a semblance of safety in numbers, so Haemonculi of like interests pool like clotting blood in its depths.

All Haemonculi see the material dimension as theirs to do with as they wish. It is a cornucopia of potentiality, a breeding ground of endless test subjects and an ocean of virgin promise in unlocking the secrets of being – a feat to humble the very gods. The Haemonculi's importance to the Drukhari race is assured by their people's spiralling depravity, and so the Covens are free to indulge in every wicked interest they can conceive in the profusion of lairs that cluster at Commorragh's underside. These Covens compete with one another for the spoils of raids, eager to advance their gruesome society's vision of degradation. They also clash over patronage rights, or the fate of a particularly valued arena combatant – facts that the Kabals and Wych Cults ever seek to lever to their own advantage.

THE DARK CREED

Fear is a fundamental force of the universe, so the twisted clan of the Dark Creed preach, and it is one the members of their Coven claim to have harnessed. Every fiend that stalks from their flesh-pods is truly terrifying, sculpted to conform to a dark aesthetic that is considered of paramount importance. The snuffing out of life via terrifying and esoteric means from afar is viewed by the Dark Creed as the height of sophistication. The Deimographers of the Coven are much in demand, as the architects of bespoke assassinations that induce heart-stopping terror, unable to be traced back to the murder's sponsor. The Haemonculi of the Dark Creed's preference for unusual and horrific deaths has fed their compulsion for regular pacts with the shadowy Mandrakes. Though it costs the Coven a fortune in captives – alongside more unusual demands from those otherworldly terrors – the Dark Creed's masters pay willingly enough, for the allegiance of creatures that seem all but composed of raw fear is too tantalising to resist.

THE COVEN OF TWELVE

Blade-laden butchers and internecine back-stabbers of the highest order, Haemonculi of the Coven of Twelve have evolved through an unnatural process into an especially prideful faction of red-handed blademasters. The bloody sect maintain a limited membership of eleven Haemonculi, with one seat of their council ceremonially kept free in an open invitation to Urien Rakarth. Advancement to a position of power can only be achieved through disposal – via especially thorough means – of the one the aspirant seeks to succeed.

This brutal system has bred a ruthless mindset in the Coven's legions of Wracks – who seek to kill their way to the top – and the Haemonculi themselves as they administer punishments without warning, forever wary of betrayal. Their quest to stay one step ahead of each other, seeking to exploit the slightest sign of weakness, is unleashed upon their luckless foes during realspace raids, and has even seeped – via some psychotic osmosis – into the semi-sentient minds of the Twelve's most monstrous creations.

THE BLACK DESCENT

With the patience of aeons and the instincts of a hunting arachnid, the Coven of the Black Descent lays its plans and spreads its webs. Its traps and snares have won high praise from those Wych Cults whose arenas now resound with surprised screams, yet such gaudy devices are only worthy of those with limited attentions and deep pockets.

Members of the Black Descent weave ploys of feigned flights and baited ambushes, exquisitely apposite punishments for those who cross them and stratagems sometimes a thousand years in the making. Their meticulously planned realspace raids typically lure the Coven's foes to a predetermined site, chosen perhaps for some dark irony utterly lost on the lesser creatures they hunt, but also laden with traps of diabolical inventiveness. Often, storms of neurolightning selectively fry their enemies' cortices, or time-delayed mutagens cause native flora to erupt in showers of thorns that shred the awaiting defenders. Archons who wish to accompany their raids with such delights often make pacts with the Black Descent, but in doing so must take care not to inadvertently offend the Coven's overly decorous and sensitive Haemonculi.

THE HEX

Since its creation in the dark days following the Fall, the Hex has specialised in the fabrication of curses. Most of these are the product of baleful technologies whose effects have been refined to the point where – in the eyes of primitive races – they are alike to magic. Some of the Coven's favourite curses truly border on the supernatural. It was the Hex that harnessed the Plague of Glass – a pandemic that once swept the Dark City, turning its victims to statues of crystal.

Members of the Hex consider themselves the pre-eminent artists of flesh. Their

studies led to the development of the arcane rifle that bears their name and, to this day, the hexrifle is the preferred weapon of discerning assassins. Its deadly payloads have reduced a string of high-profile targets across the galaxy to little more than artistic curios.

THE EVERSPIRAL

Treading the twisting path of unholy depravity is something of a crusade for the Haemonculi of the Everspiral. They seek to make every day of existence appreciably viler, not only for individuals, but also for entire species. In fact, their ambition reaches to encompass the misery of the galaxy itself. The Everspiral seeds healthy stars with tainted energies – turning their life-giving light into a tumour-inducing glare – subtly realign planets so that their feral populaces'

astrological scryings tell horrifying new prophecies of doom, and even cross-breed xenos horrors with creatures seeping up from shadow dimensions.

Members of the Everspiral are the most committed of all Haemonculi to a headlong plunge into depravity, believing themselves deified by their acts of despicable predation. However, they demand more anguish to avoid slipping into a shadow existence than their fellow Covenites, and utilise large numbers of Cronos Parasite Engines to better supply the substance of suffering they require.

THE EBON STING

The Coven of the Ebon Sting is renowned for its exceptionally well-made Talos. Each of these multi-limbed Pain Engines combine the Ebon Sting's fleshcrafting

art with its peerless efficiency, resulting in several subtypes that have proliferated only within this Coven's network. From the revolting Black Jester – of which only a single, fratricidal example remains – to the trio of many-bladed Iron Dervishes and the suspiciously autonomous Polythyst, the Ebon Sting's artisanal creations are in high demand on the battlefield, in the arena and for private performances.

Yet it is for its forcibly administered tinctures and potions that the Coven is truly feared. The weapons of its Talos are coated in the Ebon Sting's signature toxin. Derived from the flesh of the worm-like nichtovermid, the elixir causes its victim's flesh to harden into a chitinous cocoon – a chrysalis that nurtures the next generation of nichtovermids inside the conscious host.

DARK DISCIPLINES

Within each Coven of Haemonculi, several broad schools of nightmarish thought exist. These disciplines cross Coven boundaries, flourishing and fading like midnight blooms as fashions ebb and flow. Sometimes, one particular discipline will be prevalent within a Coven, or sometimes several contradictory traditions exist concurrently, only to be replaced by others as the millennia come and go. It is tacitly recognised that a Coven with specialists in many fields benefits from a greater symbiosis with the many and varied needs of the Dark City.

Among the many devotees to such disciplines are the Nemesines – individuals who commit their depraved intellects to seeking the death-secrets of every sentient being – while Ever-Nemesines attempt to wipe out ephemeral phenomena such as joy or enlightenment. Black Cornucopians are flesh collectors and hoarders, while Nadirists and Masters of Apotheosis each seek a kind of corrupted godhood – one of dark creation, the other of evil incarnate.

FEALTY'S PRICE

Where loyalty exists in Drukhari society, it is a fluid and malleable commodity. The acquisition of personal power, the need to dominate lesser individuals and the desire to fulfil every decadent whim mean there is no shortage of those willing to sell their blades for a price.

Commorragh plays host to many of the galaxy's most villainous individuals, including alien mercenaries, bounty hunters, corsairs and renegades, all risking their souls in the hopes of claiming the riches of the Dark City. Yet for each band of xenos scum that conglomerates in Commorragh are countless more self-serving Drukhari, aiming to secure their own foothold and prosper under the dark shadow of Vect's dominion.

Some are highly organised commercial and military enterprises, such as Kabals without territory who have survived their peers and now profit from their expertise by hiring their assets out to rival cliques. Others may be loose bands of individuals drawn together by aligned passions or patrons. A number of these offer specialised battlefield skills, as well as a deniable detachment for canny Archons seeking anonymous assassinations. Some also form an interstitial layer within the fractal social complexity of the Dark City's interconnected realms.

SCOURGES

Among the twisted prongs of Commorragh's spires and jutting spurs, dark shapes can sometimes be seen flitting to and fro. These are the Scourges, soaring and hedonistic warriors whose flesh and bones are remoulded with wings grafted onto their anatomy. Such Drukhari have surrendered themselves to the foul surgeries and agonies of the Haemonculi and emerged from their laboratories as avian hunters, masters of the Dark City's upper reaches.

Scourges fulfil a vital role in Commorragh's endless politicking, intrigue and murderous bargaining. Despite their incredibly advanced technology, no Archon can be certain that messages will not be intercepted or subtly altered, and psychic communication is utterly forbidden. Instead, the powerful of the Dark City pay handsomely for Scourges to take their missives by hand. Each communiqué is sealed with tailor-made poisons for which the antidote, – in theory – is held by the intended recipient, to ensure the Scourges are not tempted by a rival to delay or divert the message. So

important are Scourges to the networks of communication, that to kill one invites the wrath of Commorragh's powerful lords down upon the perpetrator with unbridled excess.

With bones drilled hollow, bands of new muscle blended with their own and adrenaline dispensers – among many other esoteric additions – Scourges have become far removed from other Drukhari. Some seek ever more bizarre bio-enhancements, especially the veterans known as Solarites. Many grow needle-fine quills from their scalp, have their skulls elongated or their eyesight sharpened to pinpoint the merest movement of prey at great distances. With the wealth that a skilled Scourge can obtain from the paranoid elite of Commorragh, they equip themselves with expensive and exquisite wargear. Their ghostplate armour is supple and porous, shot through with pockets of lighter-than-air gas that accentuate their natural grace. This armour also projects a personal force field, capable of scattering even withering hails of fire on those occasions their prey can land a shot.

Protective of their expensively altered bodies, Scourges prefer to engage their foe at range, and their keen eyesight allows them to savour the injuries they inflict in exquisite detail. Their weapons are designed to be fired on the wing, allowing Scourges to unleash punishing barrages before swiftly redeploying. Many carry shardcarbines, an advanced development of the splinter weapons favoured by the Kabals. Aided by finely calibrated suspensors, Scourges also wield a variety of other armaments tailored to their victims. Heat lances spear through the mechanical contrivances of weaker races with beams of blistering energy, while shredders entangle masses of screaming soldiers in clouds of razor-sharp monofilament wire. Scourges are highly sought after on realspace raids by those who can afford their price, though there are many others vying for a raid orchestrator's attention.

COURTS OF THE ARCHONS

Archons surround themselves with a coterie of favoured retainers, emulating – consciously or not – the depraved nobility that once ruled the

Dark City, before the rise of Vect. These Courts of mercenaries, bodyguards and status symbols can vary widely, depending on the fleeting needs and shifting personality of the Kabalite lord or lady on whom they attend.

The Lhamaeans are members of the mysterious sisterhood of Lhilitu, and they are masters in the skill of crafting and administering poisons. They concoct some of the most potent toxins in use throughout Commorragh. A mere scratch from a Lhamaean's shaimeshi blade can cause a victim's flesh to begin eating itself. Different distillations cause the brain to swell and crack the skull, blood to acidify or organs to rupture.

When an Archon conducts a realspace raid, they may also be accompanied by a chained slave-being that is host to a strange creature of the Webway – a Medusae. These highly empathic parasites feed on dreams and nightmares, and resemble a collection of tendrilled brains clamped upon their host. Meeting the gaze of a Medusae can cause instant emotional haemorrhaging, and Archons employ these hybrid creatures for their ability to absorb the roiling sensations of the battlefield. When consumed, the bulbous brain-fruit they grow can bring back all the vivid emotions of a raid.

It is not only Drukhari that Archons employ. In the depths of Commorragh lies the district of Sec Maegra. Alien mercenaries are found here in profusion, competing fiercely for lucrative murder-contracts. Among them are the Sslyth – serpentine bodyguards more reliable than many treacherous Drukhari. This multi-armed race fell to the temptations of excess millennia ago, and many now ply their trade in the Dark City. Their swift reflexes, arsenal of weapons and insensibility to high levels of pain make them ideal interceptors of enemies, both on the battlefield and within the Archon's own domain.

Ur-Ghuls, meanwhile, are hideous, sightless aliens that haunted the ziggurats of Shaa-dom before that sub-realm's destruction. Still found in dark corners across the galaxy, each Ur-Ghul is an agile predator that hunts using the rows of quivering scent-pits banding its face, above maws of needle-like teeth. They are highly prized as entertainments, being fed choice slaves before select audiences, but are also used as advance detectors of approaching assassins.

MANDRAKES
All manner of nightmarish creatures prowl through Commorragh's twisted realms. A great

many tracts of the city are avoided, feared by Drukhari for the predatory horrors that dwell within. Yet nowhere is more shrouded with dread than Aelindrach, for here darkness itself seems to have gained a sort of sentience. Aelindrach is the home realm of the Mandrakes – sinister Drukhari who can pull themselves into reality through another being's shadow. The Mandrakes' skin writhes with sickly, illuminated runes, and they clothe themselves in the leathery flesh of their victims. Their disturbing faces shift and flow, featureless one moment and split by a fang-filled maw the next.

Mandrakes exist simultaneously in reality and a cursed otherworld. They are not entirely corporeal; shots and blows sometimes pass through their body as if it were smoke. They are able to manifest anywhere that shadows pool, dragging themselves up with sinewy strength and reaching for luckless victims with filth-encrusted claws. Though some Commorrites claim the Mandrakes descend from a baleful union between ancient Aeldari and unholy entities, others maintain they are the remnants of a forbidden Cult that found its own way to survive the Fall. Some have even whispered they are one's own reflections, crawling from mirror dimensions to consume their creators. All such tales reflect the Mandrakes' disturbing reality. Their dark skin seems to absorb light rather than reflect it, they are surrounded by a chill aura of shadow that saps the warmth from the air and their ice-cold grip freezes the skin. The sigils of destruction carved into their flesh pulse when the Mandrakes feed upon the pain and terror of their prey, and the creatures can channel this freezing energy into a blast of cold fire.

Their ability as consummate shock troops – emerging behind enemy lines, inside starships or even locked rooms – make them highly valued by the cruel masters of the Dark City. Yet many fear to seek them out, for their esoteric price cannot be evaded. Usually, Mandrakes demand slaves that they take away to an unknown fate in Aelindrach. Sometimes, they will ask for something more exotic, such as a heartbeat, a true name, or a final breath. Arrogant lords who renege on such bargains do not last long, for Mandrakes are notorious for their ability to track down any quarry. Sealed in an impenetrable fastness, surrounded by the most expensive bodyguards or hidden behind subdimensional barriers, nowhere is safe. Sooner or later, a cold claw will reach from the darkness, and the icy bite of the Mandrake is never far behind.

INCUBI SHRINES

The Incubi, dwelling in sacred shrines, dedicate their entire existence to war alone. They are sublimely skilled warriors who spend countless hours perfecting the art of the killing strike. Despite their puritanical and austere way of life, this produces no virtue in them. At the core of their bloodstained souls they desire to kill as many enemies as possible, as often as possible.

Each Incubus fights in an incredibly advanced warsuit of menacing appearance and strength. It is so perfectly designed that it serves as a second skin, the segments flowing over one another like silk, whilst resisting the most powerful strikes of the foe – whether at range or in close quarters. Such is the perfection of its fit and forging, the warsuit makes no noise when its wearer walks.

The Incubi consider their weapons, klaives and demiklaives, to be the true weapons. These heavily-bladed swords can be wielded with one or two hands and are incredibly light. They can be swung by an expert in tight, controlled arcs as well as broad, beheading sweeps. Their sharp blades are wreathed in dark energy that separates all matter through which they pass at a molecular level, meaning that conventional armour offers little protection from the Incubi's precise cuts – such is the Incubi's training that no foe, even monstrous beast or armoured vehicle, is safe from them. Though they are supremely gifted duellists, the Incubi have no real concept of honour. They train in numerous ways of combat and will gladly kill a foe in the most efficient way possible.

Such is the importance of klaives to the Incubi that their leaders – the Klaivex – are named for them. To earn this rank and to be a champion of the elite requires an Incubus to achieve immense mastery of the klaive, regardless of which shrine a Klaivex belongs to. For example, in the Shrine of Naked Hatred, a potential leader must defeat the incumbent in single combat, and then flay the defeated with only four strokes of the blade. Should they fail, they themselves are skinned with their own klaive. Within the Shrine of the Sublime Murder, the potential champion must fight unarmoured – with one arm tied behind their back – against four giant captives, such as Tyranid Warriors, Go'menka or

Space Marines clad in power armour and wielding whichever Imperial close combat weapons they choose. For those who desire to be Klaivex among the Incubi of the Shrine of the Frozen Void, they must travel alone to three death worlds, each densely populated with predatory megafauna. They are required to return with the dozen barbed tentacles of a dodekafex, the ceramite-hard beak of a tyranosquid and the head of a colossal land shark. Those that return with any of these prize trophies missing are sold to the Haemonculi, with whom a fate most grim awaits them.

The obsidian shrines in which the Incubi dwell and practice their murderous arts are menacing places, with an iron statue of Khaine – the ancient Aeldari god of murder – at their very centre. They are ruled over by humourless Hierarchs, warriors of such formidable skill and terrifying reputations that they wield immense political influence, despite relatively small holdings in Commorragh compared to the greatest Kabals. The reputation of the Incubi is such that patrons and aspirants continuously flock to these locales, wishing to learn or hire the murderous arts of their order. The process of becoming an Incubus is long, gruelling and unforgiving. Those deemed weak are slaughtered, their burnt remains serving as an offering to Khaine and placed at his statue. Those deemed strong grow hardened, prosper and learn. The only true way to become an Incubus is to become skilled enough to best one in combat and seize their armour, and even when the hopeful has accomplished this most difficult task, they must complete one much more depraved and spiteful. The aspirant must kill an Aspect Warrior of the Asuryani in single combat, shatter their precious spirit stone and hand it to their shrine's Hierarch. The rent gemstone is rebuilt into a psychic torture device called a tormentor and mounted on the new Incubus' chest, from which an aura

of evil and fear emanates that penetrates the psyches of even the most indomitable enemies. It is of little surprise that the Incubi have earned the undying hatred of the Asuryani as an entire race, and even those among the Aspect Warriors who have never lost a brother or sister of their shrines to these merciless Drukhari long to slay them.

The Incubi have immense resources, accumulated from fighting for Archons – and occasionally Succubi and Haemonculi – for millennia, which they hoard jealously. Few outside the shrines have any idea what these elite warriors do with their vast wealth, but all is put to use with the same efficiency as to the wielding of their blades. They have their

The Archon with whom I am in covenant pays me to kill her enemies. Before her, there were others who paid me to kill their enemies, and after her there others still. As long as I am paid I do not betray those who pay me – but when a covenant is concluded, I go wherever Khaine wills.

DRAZHAR, MASTER OF BLADES

Even amongst the insular ranks of the Incubi, the enigmatic Drazhar remains a mystery. All that is known of his origins is that he entered the Great Shrine of the Incubi unannounced and unbidden, clad in the segmented armour of a senior member of the Incubus creed. He cut his way into the inner sanctum and slew the Hierarch himself. No Incubus knew who Drazhar was, or recognised his unique battle gear. All that anyone knew was that he never lost a duel, yet never expressed a desire to be a Klaivex or Hierarch. Thus, Drazhar has become the Executioner – the champion of his order. He never speaks and has never removed his helmet. Even his name is ceremonial, meaning 'living sword'. His heart is unblemished by emotion and pride, and he exists only to kill. Such is the example he sets, those Incubi who fight alongside him put aside their jealousies and rivalries and are driven to fight to the very extremes of their martial expertise.

own networks of spies and informers, for more than one Archon has sought to rob an Incubi shrine of its riches and wargear in the past. The knowledge the Incubi gather enables them to prepare for combat with their fellow Drukhari, as they learn the habits and ways of Kabals they may be employed to fight against. Crucially, their intelligence ensures that they never fight for a side that is doomed to lose an inter-Kabal war, and therefore avoid throwing away their lives needlessly.

The Incubi are mercenaries, willing to fight for anyone at any time. They are so disciplined that some whisper they can even be trusted to keep their word. As such, their value as bodyguards and shock troops is unparalleled. They gladly join Drukhari raiding forces – provided they are rewarded adequately – taking a cold joy in proving their skill at war and taking the opportunity to kill on battlefields all over realspace. When the fight is joined, the Incubi frequently lead the Drukhari assault,

ARHRA, THE FALLEN PHOENIX

Arhra was the Father of Scorpions. He was the first Exarch of the Striking Scorpions Aspect Warriors of the Asuryani, and left an indelible mark on their practices that persists to this day. He was their Phoenix Lord, the most sinister of all those majestic warriors, but he turned against his kin, and the Aeldari believe that he burned with the dark light of Chaos. There are rare occasions when the Phoenix Lords find themselves on opposing sides in war, in conflicts known as *las'raichan bhlàrmhori* – approximately meaning 'battle of the undying' – and Arhra has been involved in two of them. Few have any idea what has happened to the Fallen Phoenix. Some whisper that he lives in the webway still, continuing to teach his murderous ways. Rumours persist of an epic, seventeen-day duel between Arhra and Karandras – the Phoenix Lord of the Striking Scorpions – in the devastated ruins of Craftworld Zandros. Some even say that Drazhar himself was once Arhra, but few have any idea. Those that do refuse to speak of such matters.

however, particularly wealthy Archons and Overlords pay them to serve as rearguards – though for such a role the Incubi charge a great deal more. That is what it takes to prevent these mercenaries indulging their deep desire for murderous violence. Such is the reputation of the Incubi and their sinister Executioner, Drazhar, that even Vect himself brings them into his employ for tasks of the greatest importance. The Supreme Overlord demanded the Incubi slay Yvraine, leader of the Ynnari. Though they ultimately failed in this task, in the battle that ensued, Drazhar once again proved his total supremacy by striking down Jain Zar – Phoenix Lord of the Howling Banshees Aspect Warriors.

A SINISTER SPECTACLE

Many of the multitudinous factions within the Dark City mirror their domain's nature by wearing tenebrous hues, while others indulge their hedonistic passions with clashing neons or sprays of crimson blood. Sigils of ownership or temporary fealty scar their wargear or are worn as tattoos, and many sport grisly trophies torn from their victims or preserved as mocking salutes to fallen foes.

In the moments between a raiding party's shocking assault and their foes' collapse, their victims perceive them as varying wildly in appearance. It is no wonder such attacks have given rise to twisted fairy tales and stories of nightmares made real. The Kabalites of Commorragh's martial powerhouses follow the whims of the Archon to whom their service is tied. Their sharp-edged armour is designed to intimidate and unnerve, and their blade-prowed attack craft bear identical liveries that declare their lord's power – as much to rival raiding parties as to terrified enemies. The Wyches of the gladiatorial cults wear bodygloves often stained in bold colours, the better for appreciative audiences to recognise their skill in the arena. The gloom of Commorragh breeds pallid complexions, though the skin of some is red raw, shadow black or artificially tinctured to induce fear. Many raiders – notably the misshapen creations of the Haemonculi and the horrors that are Mandrakes – fight in little more than filthy robes or layers of flayed skin, their weapons flecked with viscera and seeping with kaleidoscopic toxins.

Colours of the Kabals
Some of the heraldries employed by the ruthless Kabals have been maintained since before the time of the Fall. Others reflect the changing tastes of their rulers or the imposition of a new order when the old dynasty fell. Although all the warriors of a Kabal will share the principal colours dictated by their master, they are rarely applied in rigid uniformity.

Warriors within a given unit, particularly those with (or seeking) power, individualise their wargear in displays of wealth and skill. The number of jagged spurs in their tabards, the style and positioning of their lord's sigil and many other flourishes denote a warrior's standing within the Kabal's hierarchies. This practice is encouraged not only to stimulate competition among an Archon's followers, but also so that individuals can be more readily identified should they ever attempt an anonymous betrayal.

Kabalite Warrior of the Kabal of the Black heart

Kabalite Warrior of the Kabal of the Baleful Gaze

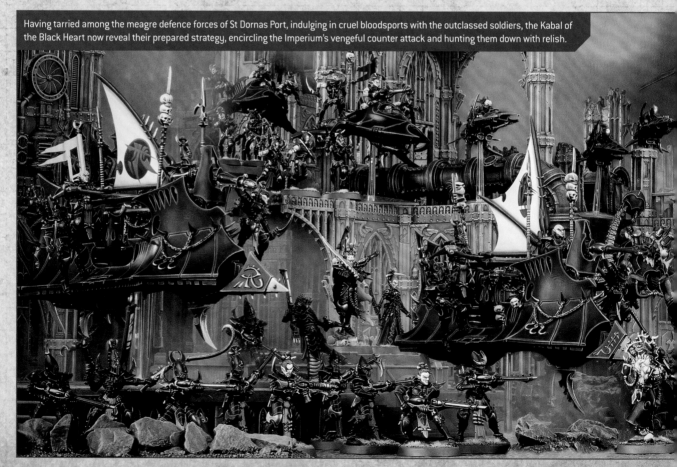

Having tarried among the meagre defence forces of St Dornas Port, indulging in cruel bloodsports with the outclassed soldiers, the Kabal of the Black Heart now reveal their prepared strategy, encircling the Imperium's vengeful counter attack and hunting them down with relish.

Kabalite Warrior of the
Kabal of the Poisoned Tongue

Sybarite of the
Kabal of the Flayed Skull

Kabalite Warrior of the
Kabal of the Obsidian Rose

Kabalite Warrior of the
Lords of the Iron Thorn

Kabalite Warrior of the
Kabal of the Last Hatred

Kabalite Warrior of the
Kabal of the Broken Sigil

The bonded Kabalites and raid-craft of Archon Vestartha bleed the remnants of the Cadian 163rd infantry regiment dry, penetrating the Guardsmen's final, weakened defences as the exhausted and terrified soldiers witness their final setting sun.

From atop the battlements of the Scabiron Palace, the Pale Marquis of Th'renn sneeringly surveys the carnage unleashed upon his orders, while his court of mercenaries and savage creatures are ever alert to desperate enemy assassins, or even ambitious allies.

Archons are imposing figures, who display their superiority with extravagant wargear and sinister trophies of significant kills.

Haemonculi are nightmarish, living exhibits of their skills. Many boast extra limbs, bony growths and many lifetimes worth of scars.

As ostentatious killers, Succubi maintain arrays of weapons and signature accoutrements that complement their fighting styles.

Archon with splinter pistol and huskblade

Haemonculus with stinger pistol, haemonculus tools, ichor injector and scissorhand

Succubus with agoniser and archite glaive

Wyches

Sporting an exotic variety of individual fashions, Wyches still acknowledge the chosen livery of their Cult, by which their patrons can recognise them and appreciate their feats of artistry.

Wych of the Cult of Strife

Wych of the Cult of the Seventh Woe

Hekatrix of the Cult of the Blade Denied

Wych of the Cult of the Red Grief

Wych of the Cult of the Cursed Blade

With her transports and attack craft emblazoned with the Cult of Strife's sigils, Lelith Hesperax wastes no opportunity for demonstrations of her sisterhood's power, while the Queen of Knives herself grants only the choicest opponents the gift of her deadly company.

At the fringes of the airborne Floating Canopies of Xynd, a mile above the desolate surface, gangs of Hellions in the pay of the Cult of the Red Grief swarm the aerial outposts of the T'au, while the crew of their supporting Razorwing targets the outpost's anti-grav generators.

Drawn from his foul abode by the promise of a dark and rare bounty, the master fleshcrafter, Urien Rakarth, unleashes his underlings and monstrous Pain Engines among the chem-choked ziggurats of Quanta Magnifica to harvest the flesh his experiments demand.

The isolated T'au research world of Fal'skio becomes the latest to supplement the hideous collections of the Prophets of Flesh. The Coven's augmented and scar-ridden aberrants strike from outflanking Raiders while the Kroot are occupied with waves of inured thralls.

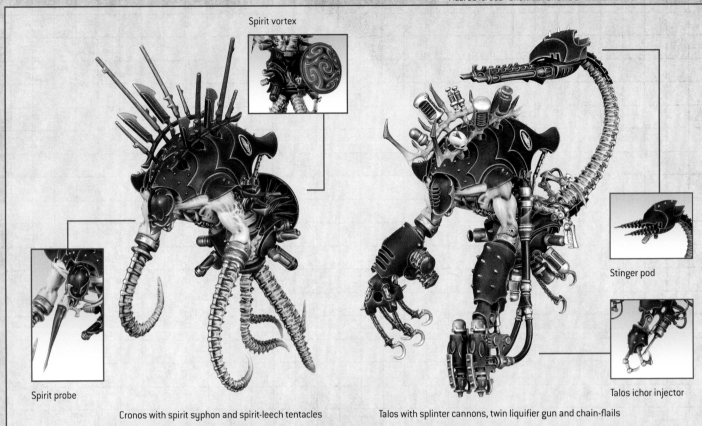

Spirit vortex

Spirit probe

Cronos with spirit syphon and spirit-leech tentacles

Stinger pod

Talos ichor injector

Talos with splinter cannons, twin liquifier gun and chain-flails

In an alliance of agony, Kabalites and Wyches coordinate their attack at the Gates of Petros in the promise of greater spoils. Competing Razorwing pilots and Ravager gunners unleash heavy fire, setting the stage for the incoming Voidraven Bombers.

Shadow-skinned Mandrakes ambush from the inky ruins of a manufactorum, while Scourges plunge from soot-stained clouds to close the trap on a Saim-Hann intervention force. The mercenaries have been instructed by their employer to acquire the craftworlders' spirit stones.

Unleashing the spiritual assault of their near-necromantic tormentors, Drazhar and his Incubi protégés leap through the ruins of ancient Zandros, their giant klaives describing great, bloody arcs as they cut through their despised craftworld kin.

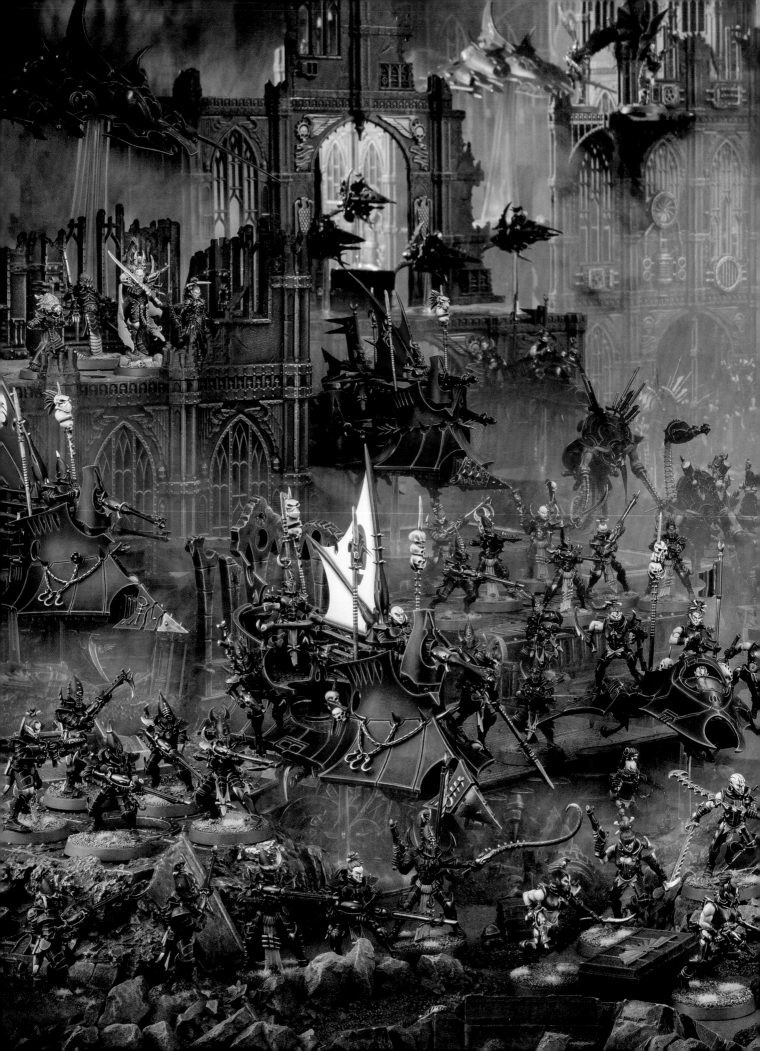

THE RULES

Welcome to the rules section of *Codex: Drukhari*. On the following pages you will find all the rules content you need to bring the multifarious Drukhari to life on the tabletop, whether it is the cruel and haughty Kabalites, athletic but murderous Wych Cults, sinister and bizarre Haemonculus Covens or a raiding force of all three. Maybe you're inspired to dive straight into some open play games, maybe you want to forge your own tales of glory and infamy with narrative play, or perhaps you can't wait to pit yourself against your opponents in nail-biting matched play contests. Whichever appeals to you – even if it's a bit of all three – this section of your Codex provides a modular toolbox that allows you to get the most out of your collection.

Of course, there's no need to take it all in at once! Some of the content on the following pages – things like your army's datasheets and the rules for its weapons – will be useful no matter what kind of game you're playing. Others, such as your army's Stratagems, Warlord Traits and Relics, will become relevant once you start playing games with Battle-forged armies. Then there's content like Lords of Commorragh and Favoured Retinues, which you will unlock by including particular models in your tabletop army. In each case, you can include these new elements at your own pace; whether you're a brand new hobbyist playing your first few games or a veteran general ready to cause carnage, there's plenty here to provide you with countless hours of fresh and exciting gameplay.

On top of this, the Drukhari are the only faction in Warhammer 40,000 with access to Power From Pain, which allows your sadistic murderers to draw power and enhance their abilities by feeding on the terror of their victims. You will find everything you need on the following pages to include these rules in your games of Warhammer 40,000, not to mention bespoke content for your Drukhari Crusade force. Included in the latter are exciting Requisitions that enable you to bring elite retinues to your force or see your nobles stave off the assassination attempts of their rivals as they ascend to the top of Commorrite society. You will also find a bespoke system allowing your Archon to barter the spoils of their raids to bring more and more regions of the Dark City under their influence, taking advantage of the many varied resources they can provide to their armies.

BATTLE-FORGED RULES

DETACHMENT ABILITIES (PG 49-52)

Units in Drukhari Detachments gain additional abilities to better reflect how their armies operate together and wage war on the battlefield. In addition, certain character models in your Drukhari army can be upgraded, increasing their abilities and also allowing you to add their elite retinues of troops to your army. You can find out more about Detachment abilities in the Battle-forged Armies section of the Warhammer 40,000 Core Book.

DRUKHARI KABALS, CULTS AND COVENS (PG 53-65)

Kabals, Wych Cults and Haemonculus Covens gain access to power abilities, including Obsessions, that represent their individual fighting styles.

STRATAGEMS (PG 68-70)

Drukhari armies have access to unique battlefield strategies and tactics that they can utilise to best their foes in any theatre of war; these are represented by the Stratagems in this section, which you can spend Command points to use in your games. You can find out more about Stratagems and Command points in the Warhammer 40,000 Core Book.

MATCHED PLAY RULES

CHAPTER APPROVED RULES (PG 71)

If you are playing a battle that instructs you to select secondary objectives, then you will be able to choose from the Drukhari ones printed here that represent tactical goals unique to their armies. You can find out more about selecting secondary objectives in many matched play mission packs, including the Eternal War mission pack found in the Warhammer 40,000 Core Book.

ARMY RULES

WARLORD TRAITS (PG 72-73)

The Warlord of a Drukhari army can have one of the traits presented in this section. These help to personalise the leader of your force and better reflect their individual combat prowess and command style on the battlefield.

RELICS (PG 74-75)

Drukhari leaders can take powerful devices of torture and deadly weapons called Artefacts of Cruelty into battle; these Relics and the rules they bestow are described in this section.

CRUSADE RULES

CRUSADE (PG 76-87)

Drukhari have access to a host of additional rules that enhance your Crusade experience and further personalise your Crusade force. These include bespoke Agendas, Requisitions, Battle Traits and Crusade Relics that reflect the rich background of Drukhari armies. Amongst the rules presented in this section are Raid Spoils, a brand new type of Resource that Drukhari can collect and spend to gain new territories within Commorragh.

DATASHEETS

DATASHEETS (PG 88-113)

This section is essential to all Drukhari players, regardless of preferred play style, containing as it does the datasheets for Drukhari units. Each datasheet describes, among other things, the profiles of its models, the wargear they can be equipped with and the abilities they have. You can find out more about datasheets in the Warhammer 40,000 Core Book.

POINTS

POINTS VALUES (PG 114-115)

If you are playing a game that uses points values, you can use the alphabetised lists in this section to determine the cost of each unit from your army. These values will be reviewed and updated annually.

WARGEAR

WEAPON PROFILES (PG 116-118)

This section provides an alphabetised list of Drukhari specific weapons featured in this Codex in one handy reference, and should be used in conjunction with the datasheets section.

RULES REFERENCE

GLOSSARY (PG 119)

In this section you will find a glossary of rules terms used in this Codex. This is intended to work alongside the glossary found in the Warhammer 40,000 Core book, and aid in resolving any complex rules interactions that may arise.

REFERENCE (PG 120)

Here you will find a handy bullet-pointed rules reference that summarises some common Drukhari rules.

COMBAT PATROL

Combat Patrol is the smallest size game, and the Drukhari force below is a great way to start – regardless of whether you want to play an open play game, forge a narrative with a Crusade army or compete in a matched play mission.

Created from the contents of the Combat Patrol: Drukhari boxed set, this force can be used in a Battle-forged army and in itself comprises a Patrol Detachment, as described in the Warhammer 40,000 Core Book.

Kabalite Warriors are a reliable ranged unit that, as part of a Battle-forged army, gain the Objective Secured ability (see the Warhammer 40,000 Core Book), making them ideally suited to holding battlefield objectives. You can use them as a single large unit – which grants them additional weapon options – or as separate units of 5 models, allowing them some more flexibility to capture objectives on the battlefield.

Providing melee punch to your force is an Archon and a unit of deadly Incubi. The Archon is the mastermind of your raid, whose Overlord ability helps to magnify the already impressive melee capabilities of the Incubi, or the pinpoint shooting of your Kabalite Warriors while they are nearby.

The Raider is the Drukhari's fast transport. Able to carry your melee specialist Archon and Incubi into the heart of the enemy army, or provide a shooting platform with its Open-topped ability for your Kabalite Warriors, the Raider is a fast and flexible addition. It can also launch deadly weaponry of its own, able to get into position to use them to full effect.

The Ravager is an extremely mobile weapons platform, able to mount anti-infantry disintegrators or dark lances to punish enemy vehicles and monsters. With the speed required to avoid your opponent's anti-vehicle weapons, the Ravager is rightly feared.

DETACHMENT ABILITIES

A **Drukhari** Detachment is one that only includes models with the **Drukhari** keyword (excluding models with the **Unaligned** keyword).

- **Drukhari** Detachments gain the Raiding Forces and Weakling Kin abilities.
- If your army is Battle-forged, each **Drukhari** Detachment in your army must be designated as a Kabal Detachment, Wych Cult Detachment, Haemonculus Coven Detachment or Realspace Raid Detachment. Your army can only include one Realspace Raid Detachment. Realspace Raid Detachments gain the Realspace Raid ability.
- Troops units in **Drukhari** Detachments gain the Objective Secured ability (this ability is described in the Warhammer 40,000 Core Book).

RAIDING FORCES

The fractious animosities that pervade the Dark City are set aside when orchestrating raids upon the worlds of lesser races.

If every Detachment in your army is a **Drukhari** Patrol Detachment, change the Command Cost of those Detachments to 0CP.

- All <**Kabal**> units in a Kabal Detachment gain a Drukhari Obsession (see page 53).

- All <**Wych Cult**> units in a Wych Cult Detachment gain a Drukhari Obsession (see page 53).

- All <**Haemonculus Coven**> units in a Haemonculus Coven Detachment gain a Drukhari Obsession (see page 53).

WEAKLING KIN

While the Drukhari tolerate the presence of other Aeldari, they have little time for their kin's pitiful concerns, and cooperation between them and those they perceive as inferior is… strained at best.

- You cannot include **Drukhari** and non-**Drukhari Aeldari** units in the same Detachment unless all those units have the **Ynnari** keyword.

REALSPACE RAID

The most masterful Archons know well the value of offering a share of the spoils to attain the services of some of Commorragh's deadliest denizens.

If a Realspace Raid Detachment contains one **Archon** unit that is your **Warlord**, one **Succubus** unit and one **Haemonculus** unit, and at least one **Kabalite Warriors** unit, at least one **Wyches** unit and at least one **Wracks** unit, all units (excluding **Blades for Hire** units, unless otherwise specified) in that Detachment gain a Drukhari Obsession.

As well as gaining Drukhari Obsessions for each <**Kabal**>, <**Wych Cult**> and <**Haemonculus Coven**> unit in a Realspace Raid Detachment (see page 53), you can also select the associated Kabal, Wych Cult and Haemonculus Coven Relics for the units in that Detachment, even though your **Warlord** is not from a Wych Cult or Haemonculus Coven.

All units in a Realspace Raid Detachment gain the **Realspace Raider** keyword, and you can replace your **Warlord**'s Overlord ability with the following ability:

Raid Mastermind: While a friendly **Realspace Raider Core** unit is within 6" of this model, each time an attack is made by a model in that unit, re-roll a hit roll of 1.

LORDS OF COMMORRAGH

Over their long lifetimes, the greatest of Commorragh's denizens will often engage in a number of depraved and bizarre diversions in order to bring themselves amusement, or to slake their unnatural desires. Whether these are idle curiosities or maddened obsessions, they are invariably deadly to those who fall into their grasp, or fail to execute their will.

If your army is Battle-forged and includes any **DRUKHARI** Detachments (excluding Auxiliary Support, Super-heavy Auxiliary or Fortification Network Detachments), then when you muster your army, you can upgrade one of the following **DRUKHARI CHARACTER** units (excluding named characters) from each Detachment in your army: **ARCHON**, **SUCCUBUS**, **HAEMONCULUS**. If the Detachment is a Realspace Raid Detachment, you can upgrade one **ARCHON**, one **SUCCUBUS** and one **HAEMONCULUS** unit from that Detachment.

Make a note on your army roster each time you upgrade a unit using these rules. Each upgraded unit also gains an additional keyword, as described below:

- An upgraded **ARCHON** unit gains the **MASTER ARCHON** keyword and the Splintered Genius Kabalite Diversion, opposite.
- An upgraded **SUCCUBUS** unit gains the **MASTER SUCCUBUS** keyword and the Show Stealer Wych Cult Spectacle, opposite.
- An upgraded **HAEMONCULUS** unit gains the **MASTER HAEMONCULUS** keyword and the Alchemical Maestro Haemonculus Proclivity, opposite.

Each time you upgrade one of the aforementioned units, its Power Rating is increased, as shown in the table below. If you are playing a matched play game, or a game that uses a points limit, then the points value of that unit is also increased by the amount shown in the same table.

Your army (or Crusade force) cannot include more than one **MASTER ARCHON** unit from the same Kabal, more than one **MASTER SUCCUBUS** unit from the same Wych Cult or more than one **MASTER HAEMONCULUS** unit from the same Haemonculus Coven.

A Crusade force cannot start with any upgraded **CHARACTER** units – to include one in a Crusade force, you must use the Lord of the Dark City Requisition (pg 78).

LORDS OF COMMORRAGH

UPGRADE	POWER	POINTS
Splintered Genius	+1	+15
Show Stealer	+1	+15
Alchemical Maestro	+1	+20

KABALITE DIVERSION

SPLINTERED GENIUS
This Archon's usually calm exterior belies the truth of their debauched mind; that it is a battleground between extreme egos. Their violently sadistic side awaits only the right trigger – the fear, pain or weakness of others. Once unleashed, this Archon explodes into a killing fury, using their victims to slake their dark desires before regaining their regal composure.

Once per battle, at the end of the Fight phase, if this model is within Engagement Range of any enemy units, it can fight again.

RELICS AND WARLORD TRAITS
You can give a **MASTER ARCHON** model with this Kabalite Diversion the Soulhelm Relic, instead of giving them an Artefact of Cruelty Relic. In addition, you can give them the Consummate Weaponmaster Warlord Trait, instead of giving them another Warlord Trait.

Relic: Soulhelm
Bound within this bladed crown are fragments of spirit stones taken from slain Farseers. The trapped souls within constantly whisper maddening glimpses of potential futures, allowing a canny wearer to avoid some unfortunate fates.

The bearer has the following abilities:
- Each time an attack is made that targets the bearer, subtract 1 from that attack's hit roll.
- Each time the bearer would lose a wound, roll one D6: on a 5+, that wound is not lost.

Warlord Trait: Consummate Weaponmaster
This Archon obsesses over the perfect killing strike, spending years under the tutelage of one superlative blademaster after the next. No rival can be suffered to know the Archon's capabilities, and each mentor is disposed of once they have no skills left to impart.

Add 1 to the Damage characteristic of all melee weapons this **WARLORD** is equipped with (excluding Relics).

WYCH CULT SPECTACLE

SHOW STEALER
This master of the killing art never misses an opportunity to extend their gory displays of violence. With sublime grace, their skill demands all eyes are fixed upon their talents, leaping from dance to dance and ever seeking another encore.

Each time this model makes a consolidation move, it can move an additional 3", and it does not have to finish this move closer to the closest enemy model.

RELICS AND WARLORD TRAITS
You can give a **Master Succubus** model with this Wych Cult Spectacle the Dancer's Edge Relic, instead of giving them an Artefact of Cruelty Relic. In addition, you can give them the Whirling Death Warlord Trait, instead of giving them another Warlord Trait.

Relic: Dancer's Edge
The blade of this deceptively light polearm was gifted from the denizens of abominable Aelindrach. With every swing, contour trails of shadowy vapour hang in its wake as the blade slips, seamlessly, between the shadow realm and reality.

Model equipped with an archite glaive only. This Relic replaces an archite glaive and has the following profile:

WEAPON	RANGE	TYPE	S	AP	D
Dancer's Edge	Melee	Melee	+2	-4	2

Abilities: Each time an attack is made with this weapon, on an unmodified wound roll of 6, invulnerable saving throws cannot be taken against that attack.

Warlord Trait: Whirling Death
This murder-artist is constantly moving, their every acrobatic step accompanied by a lashing blade. They are at their most dangerous when the foe believes them surrounded, but this simply gives them more victims to practice their killing art upon.

Each time this **Warlord** fights, after any pile-in moves, until that fight is resolved, you can choose for its Attacks characteristic to be equal to 3 plus the number of enemy models that are within 2" of it.

HAEMONCULUS PROCLIVITY

ALCHEMICAL MAESTRO
Saturated with their own vile concoctions, this master of arcane philtres is expert in the creation of agonizing toxins, liquid flesh dispensers, potent growth elixirs and a host of other substances. Those who dare to strike them down witness first hand the horror of bubbling flesh sealing what should have been fatal wounds.

Once per battle, when this model is destroyed, you can choose to roll one D6 at the end of the phase instead of using any rules that are triggered when this model is destroyed. If you do so, then on a 2+, set this model back up on the battlefield as close as possible to where they were destroyed but not within Engagement Range of any enemy models, with D3 wounds remaining.

RELICS AND WARLORD TRAITS
You can give a **Master Haemonculus** model with this Haemonculus Proclivity the Poisoner's Ampule Relic, instead of giving them an Artefact of Cruelty Relic. In addition, you can give them the Twisted Animator Warlord Trait, instead of giving them another Warlord Trait.

Relic: Poisoner's Ampule
The toxic run-off in this flask was drained from several failed experiments, distilled through the entrails of living subjects. The resultant composite brew affords a unique weapon. Shattered at the feet of an enemy, one never knows what to expect – metal-eating acids, palsy-inducing fumes or perhaps lunacy-causing filaments, rendering the heroic unintelligible.

Once per battle, at the end of your Movement phase, the bearer can use this Relic. If it does so, select one enemy unit within 9" of the bearer.
- Roll one D6: on a 2+, that unit suffers D3 mortal wounds.
- Until the start of your next turn, any Aura abilities that unit has have no effect.
- Until the start of your next turn, that unit cannot be affected by the Aura abilities of friendly models.

Warlord Trait: Twisted Animator
This deranged creature is an artist when it comes to the reshaping of flesh. A few deft slices – and a liberal application of horrifying unguents – allow ruptured skin to flow like wax and reform anew, the subject lurching back to life.

In your Command phase, you can select one friendly **<Haemonculus Coven> Wrack** unit within 3" of this **Warlord**. D3 destroyed models can be added back to the unit. These models can be set up within Engagement Range of enemy units that are already within Engagement Range of that unit.

FAVOURED RETINUES

If your army includes a **Master Archon**, **Master Succubus** or **Master Haemonculus** unit, you can also use the upgrades listed below. Each time you upgrade one of these units, its Power Rating is increased, as shown in the table below. If you are playing a matched play game, or a game that uses a points limit, then the points value of that unit is also increased by the amount shown in the same table. Make a note on your army roster each time you upgrade a unit using these rules.

A Crusade force cannot start with any upgraded units – to include one in a Crusade force, you must use the Chosen of the Master Requisition (pg 78).

KABALITE TRUEBORN

In every Kabal there exists a clique of those Drukhari who view themselves as superior to their fellow Kabalites. Most often, this is the result of having been born naturally, rather than as a result of cloning or other esoteric sciences. These 'Trueborn' – as they are known – view themselves as purer, and are afforded a more prestigious position in Commorrite society. They are able to demand the very best, and learn from an early age to protect their birthright to such power.

For each **Master Archon** unit in your army, one unit of Kabalite Warriors in the same Detachment can be upgraded to Kabalite Trueborn. Kabalite Trueborn have a maximum unit size of 10, gain the **Kabalite Trueborn** keyword and have the following additional abilities:

- Models in this unit have a Ballistic Skill characteristic of 2+.
- Add 1 to the Leadership characteristic of models in this unit.
- Each time a model in this unit makes a ranged attack, you can ignore any or all hit roll and Ballistic Skill modifiers.

HEKATRIX BLOODBRIDES

In many Wych Cults, the deadliest Hekatrixes will band together to form units who answer to none but the highest authority of that Cult. Often accompanying high ranking or prestigious Succubi into battle, these paragons of the arena have mastered the killing arts, their complimentary fighting styles proving deadly to any who face them.

For each **Master Succubus** or **Lelith Hesperax** unit in your army, one unit of Wyches in the same Detachment can be upgraded to Hekatrix Bloodbrides. Hekatrix Bloodbrides have a maximum unit size of 10, gain the **Hekatrix Bloodbrides** keyword and have the following additional abilities:

- Models in this unit have a Weapon Skill characteristic of 2+.
- Add 1 to the Leadership characteristic of models in this unit.
- Each time an attack made by a model in this unit would trigger the Blade Artists ability (pg 89), the Armour Penetration characteristic of that attack is increased by 3 instead of 1.

HAEMOXYTES

Highly prized by their masters, the Haemoxytes consider themselves to be the pinnacle of the fleshcrafting art. Grafted with a bewildering array of internal augmentations derived from both Aeldari gene-stock and that of other races, they exhibit enhanced abilities, and are often tasked with particularly vital duties by their masters. Although they are viewed with disgust by other Drukhari, it is not unusual for a Wrack to viciously slay any rivals to secure a chance to become a Haemoxyte, earning a prestigious place among their masters' favoured creations.

For each **Master Haemonculus** or **Urien Rakarth** unit in your army, one unit of Wracks in the same Detachment can be upgraded to Haemoxytes. Haemoxytes have a maximum unit size of 10, gain the **Haemoxytes** keyword and have the following additional abilities:

- Improve this unit's Save characteristic and invulnerable save by 1 (to a maximum of 4+).
- Add 1 to the Leadership characteristic of models in this unit.
- Once per phase, the first time a saving throw is failed for this unit, the Damage characteristic of that attack is changed to 0.

FAVOURED RETINUES

UNIT UPGRADE	POWER	POINTS
Kabalite Trueborn	+1 per 5 models	+2/model
Hekatrix Bloodbrides	+1 per 5 models	+2/model
Haemoxytes	+1 per 5 models	+2/model

DRUKHARI KABALS, CULTS AND COVENS

Units in a **DRUKHARI** Kabal, Wych Cult, Haemonculus Coven or Realspace Raid Detachment gain access to the following rules:

KABAL, WYCH CULT AND HAEMONCULUS COVEN OBSESSIONS

All **<KABAL>**, **<WYCH CULT>** and **<HAEMONCULUS COVEN>** units (including **URIEN RAKARTH** and **LELITH HESPERAX** units) with this ability gain a Drukhari Obsession. The Obsession gained depends upon which Kabal, Wych Cult or Haemonculus Coven they are from, as shown on the following pages. If the **<KABAL>**, **<WYCH CULT>** or **<HAEMONCULUS COVEN>** unit is from one of the Kabals, Wych Cults or Haemonculus Covens named in this section, you must use the specified Drukhari Obsession. If you have created your own Kabal, Wych Cult or Haemonculus Coven, you must instead use the rules in the appropriate section to create an Obsession for them.

KABAL, WYCH CULT AND HAEMONCULUS COVEN WARLORD TRAITS

Each Kabal, Wych Cult or Haemonculus Coven has an associated Kabal, Wych Cult or Haemonculus Coven Warlord Trait. If a **<KABAL>**, **<WYCH CULT>** or **<HAEMONCULUS COVEN> CHARACTER** model from one of the Kabals, Wych Cults or Haemonculus Covens named in this section gains a Warlord Trait, they can have the relevant Kabal, Wych Cult or Haemonculus Coven Warlord Trait instead of a Warlord Trait from pages 72-73. Note that named characters must have the Warlord Traits specified on page 72.

KABAL, WYCH CULT AND HAEMONCULUS COVEN STRATAGEMS

Each Kabal, Wych Cult or Haemonculus Coven has an associated Stratagem. If your army includes a Kabal, Wych Cult or Haemonculus Coven Detachment (excluding Auxiliary Support Detachments) from one of the Kabals, Wych Cults or Haemonculus Covens named in this section, or a Realspace Raid Detachment that includes units from any of the Kabals, Wych Cults or Haemonculus Covens named in this section, you can spend Command points to use this Stratagem in addition to those on pages 68-70.

KABAL, WYCH CULT AND HAEMONCULUS COVEN RELICS

Each Kabal, Wych Cult or Haemonculus Coven has an associated Relic. If your army is led by a **<KABAL> WARLORD**, **<WYCH CULT> WARLORD** or **<HAEMONCULUS COVEN> WARLORD** model from one of the Kabals, Wych Cults or Haemonculus Covens named in this section, you can select this Relic instead of those on pages 74-75.

*Example: A Battle-forged army includes a Realspace Raid Detachment that includes an Archon (the **WARLORD**) from the Kabal of the Black Heart, a Succubus from the Cult of the Cursed Blade and a Haemonculus from the Coven of Twelve.*

*Every **KABAL OF THE BLACK HEART** unit in that Detachment gains the Thirst for Power Obsession, every **CULT OF THE CURSED BLADE** unit in that Detachment gains the Only the Strong Will Thrive Obsession and every **COVEN OF TWELVE** unit in that Detachment gains the Butchers of Flesh Obsession.*

*Because the Archon is the **WARLORD** they can be given the Labyrinthine Cunning Warlord Trait. If you spent Command points to use the Alliance of Agony or Tolerated Ambition Stratagems, this Detachment's Succubus and/or Haemonculus could be given the Treacherous Deceiver and/or Scarlet Epicurean Warlord Traits respectively.*

*Because this Detachment is a Realspace Raid, you can spend Command points to use the Agents of Vect Stratagem because your **WARLORD** is from the Kabal of the Black Heart. You can also use the Venomous Shardbombs and A Most Inventive Demise Stratagems because the Detachment includes a Succubus and a Haemonculus from the Cult of the Cursed Blade and the Coven of Twelve respectively.*

*Because the Archon is the **WARLORD**, one **KABAL OF THE BLACK HEART CHARACTER** in the army can be given the Writ of the Living Muse Relic. Because this Detachment is a Realspace Raid, you can instead (or in addition if you use the Prizes from the Dark City Stratagem) select a **COVEN OF TWELVE CHARACTER** model to have the Flensing Blade Relic and/or select a **CULT OF THE CURSED BLADE CHARACTER** model to have the Traitor's Embrace Relic.*

KABALS

KABAL OF THE BLACK HEART

Enforcers of Vect's will, the Kabal of the Black Heart are feared as the iron gauntlet that maintains his stranglehold.

OBSESSION: THIRST FOR POWER

Though by far the largest and most influential Kabal, the Black Heart has been taught by Vect to pursue ever more power.

- Units with this Obsession that have the Power From Pain ability (pg 89) treat the current battle round as being one higher than it actually is when determining what effects they gain.
- If a Realspace Raid Detachment includes a **Kabal of the Black Heart Archon**, then until the end of the battle, all **Blades for Hire** units in that Detachment that have the Power From Pain ability also treat the current battle round as being one higher than it actually is when determining what effects they gain.
- Add 1 to the Leadership characteristic of models with this Obsession.
- Each time a unit with this Obsession is selected to shoot or fight, you can re-roll one hit roll when resolving that unit's attacks.

WARLORD TRAIT: LABYRINTHINE CUNNING

The Archons of the Kabal of the Black Heart have minds like steel traps, assimilating every detail of a situation.

While this **Warlord** is on the battlefield, each time you or your opponent spends any Command points to use a Stratagem you can roll one D6 for each Command point spent: on a 6, you gain one Command point.

RELIC: WRIT OF THE LIVING MUSE

When intoned, the words of Vect embossed upon this iron tablet invigorate all who owe him fealty.

Kabal of the Black Heart Archon model only. The bearer has the following ability: '**Writ of the Living Muse (Aura):** While a friendly **Kabal of the Black Heart Core** unit is within 6" of the bearer, each time a model in that unit makes an attack, re-roll a wound roll of 1. If the bearer is a **Realspace Raider** unit, this ability also affects **Blades for Hire** units.'

AGENTS OF VECT · OCP

Kabal of the Black Heart – Strategic Ploy Stratagem

The Supreme Overlord of Commorragh develops countermeasures for every conceivable course of events.

Use this Stratagem after your opponent uses a Stratagem (excluding Command Re-roll). Until the end of the battle, the CP cost your opponent must pay to use that Stratagem again is increased by 1. This Stratagem can only be used once.

KABAL OF THE POISONED TONGUE

The insidious Kabal of Lady Aurelia Malys, the Poisoned Tongue encircle their enemies like a stalking viper, employing the subtlest of deceits before striking with venomous potency. When their schemes call for it, they apply their practised intellects to acts of outright violence, and are capable of striking down the most dauntless of foes with the vilest of poisons.

OBSESSION: THE SERPENT'S KISS

The toxin crafters of the Kabal of the Poisoned Tongue tailor their venoms to the targets of a raid, ensuring they will have the most gruesome effect on the victims' physiologies.

- Each time a model with this Obsession makes an attack with a poisoned weapon, improve the Poisoned Weapon ability of that weapon by 1 to a maximum of 2+ (e.g. Poisoned Weapon (4+) becomes Poisoned Weapon (3+)).
- If an enemy unit has any models destroyed by an attack made with a poisoned weapon by a model with this Obsession, until the end of the turn, subtract 1 from Combat Attrition tests taken for that enemy unit.

WARLORD TRAIT: TOWERING ARROGANCE

The Archons of the Kabal of the Poisoned Tongue are aloof in the extreme, having nothing but scorn for their foes. Such is the power of their conviction that their underlings will stand their ground no matter the odds.

- Each time this **WARLORD** would lose a wound as the result of a mortal wound, roll one D6: on a 5+, that wound is not lost.
- This **WARLORD** has the following ability: '**Towering Arrogance (Aura):** While a friendly **KABAL OF THE POISONED TONGUE** unit is within 6" of this **WARLORD**, each time a Combat Attrition test is taken for that unit, ignore any or all modifiers.'

RELIC: SOUL-SEEKER

The Soul-seeker fires splinters of toxic spirit stones, each of which shatters upon impact to create clouds of empaphagic vapours.

KABAL OF THE POISONED TONGUE ARCHON model equipped with a splinter pistol only. This Relic replaces a splinter pistol and has the following profile:

WEAPON	RANGE	TYPE	S	AP	D
Soul-seeker	18"	Pistol 2	2	-2	D3

Abilities: Poisoned Weapon (2+) (pg 89). Each time you select a target for this weapon, you can ignore the Look Out, Sir rule. Each time an attack is made with this weapon, the target does not receive the benefits of cover against that attack.

INSIDIOUS MISDIRECTION   2CP

Kabal of the Poisoned Tongue – Strategic Ploy Stratagem

The Kabalites of the Poisoned Tongue excel at wrong-footing their enemies before an attack is launched.

Use this Stratagem at the start of the first battle round. Select up to three **KABAL OF THE POISONED TONGUE** units from your army and redeploy them. If the mission uses the Strategic Reserves rules, any of those units can be placed into Strategic Reserves without having to spend any additional CPs, regardless of how many units are already in Strategic Reserves. If both players have abilities that redeploy units, roll off; the winner chooses who redeploys their units first.

'We are everywhere and nowhere. We speak only incontrovertible truths and are compulsive liars. We have a hand in all Commorragh's deeds but play no part. We know everything yet plead ignorance. We are the toxin in your wine, the thorn in your side and the mocking laughter in your ears, and yet we are the reliable warrior, the helping hand in times of need and the patient listener in those of woe.

We are the Poisoned Tongue… or are we?'

- Archon Xurul ka'Teren

KABALS

KABAL OF THE FLAYED SKULL

Masters of the shadowed sky, the Kabal of the Flayed Skull pour from above in massed airborne attacks, their warriors clad in the bloody red of flayed corpses. Their arrogance and daring know no bounds, and it is said they will not even deign to step foot on a world lest it be to grind their heel into their enemy's throat.

OBSESSION: SLAY FROM THE SKIES

The Kabalites of the Flayed Skull excel in aerial warfare, using their speed and manoeuvrability to harry the most elusive targets, before bringing them down with deadly volleys from their weapons.

- Each time a model with this Obsession that can **FLY** or that is embarked upon a **TRANSPORT** unit that can **FLY** makes a ranged attack, the target does not receive the benefits of Light Cover against that attack.
- Add 2" to the Move characteristic of **VEHICLE** units with this Obsession.

WARLORD TRAIT: FAMED SAVAGERY

Renowned for their savagery, the Archons of the Kabal of the Flayed Skull remove the skin from their foes' skulls before their corpses have even hit the floor.

Add 1 to this **WARLORD**'s Strength and Attacks characteristics.

RELIC: THE OBSIDIAN VEIL

Utilising the same night-shield technology as Drukhari attack craft, the Obsidian Veil projects a broad-spectrum displacement field around its bearer, surrounding them in a cloud of murky shadow.

KABAL OF THE FLAYED SKULL ARCHON model only. The bearer has a 4+ invulnerable save.

MASTERS OF THE SHADOWED SKY   1CP

Kabal of the Flayed Skull – Battle Tactic Stratagem

The Kabalites of the Flayed Skull view the skies as their rightful territory, and will scour it of those enemies who dare to trespass.

Use this Stratagem when you select a **KABAL OF THE FLAYED SKULL** unit from your army to shoot with. Until the end of the phase, each time that unit makes an attack that targets a unit that can **FLY**, add 1 to that attack's hit roll. If the target is an **AIRCRAFT** unit, add 2 to that attack's hit roll instead.

KABAL OF THE OBSIDIAN ROSE

Known for their exquisitely crafted instruments of death, every warrior of the Kabal of the Obsidian Rose is an exacting virtuoso with a reputation for perfection. No lapse in skill or ability is acceptable for these obsessive purists, as they seek ever more precise applications of murdercraft.

OBSESSION: FLAWLESS WORKMANSHIP

Every weapon produced in the workshops of the Kabal of the Obsidian Rose is a masterpiece, equal in accuracy and lethality to the finest armaments of any other Kabal.

- Add 6" to the Range characteristic of all Assault, Rapid Fire and Heavy weapons (excluding Relics) models with this Obsession are equipped with.
- Each time a unit with this Obsession is selected to shoot or fight, you can re-roll one wound roll when making that unit's attacks.

WARLORD TRAIT: DEATHLY PERFECTIONIST

The Archons of the Kabal of the Obsidian Rose are all skilled weaponsmiths, and have a reputation for perfectionism in their craftsmanship. Their personal armaments are the finest examples of their Kabal.

Add 1 to the Strength characteristic of weapons this **WARLORD** is equipped with (excluding Relics).

RELIC: THE ARMOUR OF MISERY

Crafted using psycho-empathic shards of poisoned wraithbone, this armour emanates crippling waves of dread, causing foes to quail.

KABAL OF THE OBSIDIAN ROSE ARCHON model only.

- The bearer has a Save characteristic of 3+.
- Each time a melee attack is made against the bearer, subtract 1 from that attack's hit roll.

FAILURE IS NOT AN OPTION   1CP

Kabal of the Obsidian Rose – Strategic Ploy Stratagem

Even when faced with insurmountable odds, the Kabalites of the Obsidian Rose know that anything less than the perfect execution of their deadly art is utterly unacceptable.

Use this Stratagem after taking Combat Attrition tests for a **KABAL OF THE OBSIDIAN ROSE** unit from your army, but before any models flee. You can shoot with each model that would flee. If the unit is within Engagement Range of any enemy units, each model that would flee can instead make one melee attack. If any enemy models are destroyed by these attacks, no models flee from this unit. Treat the Morale test as having been passed.

BATTLE-FORGED RULES

OTHER KABALS

If your chosen Kabal does not have an associated Kabal Obsession above, you must instead create their Kabal Obsession by selecting two of the Obsessions from the lists below. An All-consuming Obsession counts as two selections.

DARK MIRTH

This Kabal revels in the misfortunes of others. Whether lulling vengeful aggressors into minefields or panicking victims into breaking cover, the sinister chuckling of these warriors is often the last thing their victims hear.

Units with this Obsession have the following ability:

Dark Mirth (Aura): While it is within 12" of this unit, each time an enemy unit is selected to make a Normal Move, Advance, Fall Back or is selected to charge, roll one D6: on a 5+, that enemy unit suffers 1 mortal wound.

DEADLY DECEIVERS (ALL-CONSUMING)

Cruel misdirection is this Kabal's speciality, whether that is seeding the ground before them with torment mines, a feigned retreat leading the foe into an ambush or disappearing from view only to reappear unleashing a hail of deadly splinter fire.

Units with this Obsession are eligible to shoot in a turn in which they Fell Back, but if they do, then until the end of the turn, each time a model in that unit makes a ranged attack, subtract 1 from that attack's hit roll.

DISDAIN FOR LESSER BEINGS

This Kabal inhabits some of the highest spires of Commorragh, allowing them to literally look down on their rivals. Convinced of their superiority, these haughty warriors see victory as an absolute certainty, and to flee before their lessers is all but unthinkable.

Each time a Combat Attrition test is taken for a unit with this Obsession, add 1 to that Combat Attrition test.

MERCILESS RAZORKIN

The perfection of tailored fault lines in their crystalline ammunition is a speciality of this Kabal. Fracturing under stress an instant before they hit, these shards shower enemies in a storm of toxin-laced shrapnel.

Each time a model with this Obsession makes an attack with a splinter weapon (pg 116), an unmodified hit roll of 6 scores 1 additional hit.

TORTUROUS EFFICIENCY

This Kabal have long been experts in hitting armour seals, rebreather units, fuel lines and other weak points at range. Capable of pinpointing such frailties even on the move, these marksmen vie with one another to cause the maximum pain in the most efficient manner.

Each time a model with this Obsession makes an attack with a ranged weapon, on an unmodified wound roll of 6, improve the Armour Penetration characteristic of that attack by 1.

MOBILE RAIDERS

This Kabal revels in high-speed warfare, riding superior grav-craft to battle so as to ensure they reach the foe before their erstwhile allies. It is said that even the Reaver gangs of Commorragh are envious of the swiftness of this Kabal's craft.

Add 2" to the Move characteristic of models with this Obsession that can **FLY**.

SOUL BOUND

This Kabal has studied the process of dying for countless centuries, experimenting with binding souls to corpses in the hopes of mastering the transition between life and death.

Each time a model with this Obsession would lose a wound as a result of a mortal wound, roll one D6: on a 5+, that wound is not lost.

TOXIN CRAFTERS (ALL-CONSUMING)

This Kabal is a manufacturer and distributor of many lethal poisons, but they are careful to always maintain a large stockpile of their most potent toxins for their own nefarious use.

- Each time a model with this Obsession makes an attack with a poisoned weapon, on an unmodified hit roll of 6, change that attack's Poisoned Weapon ability to Poisoned Weapon (2+).
- Each time a model with this Obsession makes an attack with a poisoned weapon, re-roll a wound roll of 1.

TWISTED HUNTERS

Selective predators one and all, this Kabal's warriors compete to acquire the rarest and choicest trophies. The index finger of a devout Canoness, the bleached skull of a T'au Commander or the bony crest of a Tyranid alpha beast – among other mementos – all serve to increase the warrior's prestige within the Dark City.

Each time a model with this Obsession makes an attack against a **CHARACTER** unit, add 1 to that attack's hit roll.

WEBWAY RAIDERS

The warriors of this Kabal are experts at using multiple webway portals to appear from unexpected quarters. Their enemies find themselves suddenly beset on all sides by swift and deadly fighters.

Each time you use the Webway Portal Stratagem (pg 69), if any units with this Obsession are selected, reduce the Command point cost of that Stratagem by 1.

WYCH CULTS

CULT OF STRIFE

Having risen to the apex of power through the mastery of elegant excruciation, the Cult of Strife's arenas attract more patrons than any of their rivals, and it is both in these arenas and on the battlefields of realspace that the Cult's reputation for excessive violence is writ large. They forge a spectacle of every conflict, never failing to leave their onlookers or their victims breathless.

OBSESSION: THE SPECTACLE OF MURDER

Whether enthralling spectators in the arena or slaughtering their way through an enemy army, the Cult of Strife have developed a penchant for bombastically violent opening manoeuvres, always striving to ensure they get the honour of striking the first blow.

- At the start of the Fight phase, if a unit with this Obsession is within Engagement Range of any enemy units, it can fight first that phase.
- Each time you declare a charge for a unit with this Obsession, if there are no other units from your army within Engagement Range of any of the enemy units selected as targets of that charge, add 1 to the charge roll.

WARLORD TRAIT: BLOOD DANCER

The Succubi of the Cult of Strife are renowned for their expertise at close-quarters combat within the arenas of Commorragh. The skills they display before the baying crowds on the blood-soaked sands are equally as deadly on the battlefield.

Each time this **WARLORD** makes a melee attack, an unmodified hit roll of 6 scores 2 additional hits.

RELIC: THE PHIAL BOUQUET

Worn decoratively on the wrist or shoulder, the Phial Bouquet contains a cocktail of artisanal combat drugs, decanted into the Succubus' spinal column over the course of a battle.

CULT OF STRIFE SUCCUBUS model only. Roll one D6 at the start of each battle round. Until the end of the battle round, the bearer gains the associated effect from the Combat Drugs ability table (pg 89). This effect can be one that the bearer is already affected by and is cumulative.

NO METHOD OF DEATH BEYOND OUR GRASP   2CP

Cult of Strife – Battle Tactic Stratagem

The Cult of Strife are well versed in every conceivable method of murder, and after completing one act of slaughter they will often showcase another from their repertoire.

Use this Stratagem at the end of your Shooting phase or the Fight phase. Select one **CULT OF STRIFE WYCHES** unit from your army. If it is the Shooting phase, that unit can shoot again. If it is the Fight phase, and that unit is within Engagement Range of any enemy units, that unit can fight again. You can only use this Stratagem once per battle round.

CULT OF THE CURSED BLADE

The Cursed Blade thrive on the mistrust and treachery at the heart of their own Cult, seeing betrayal as the ultimate tenet for honing their deadly arts. Woe comes swiftly to those who accept the welcoming smile and hand of friendship offered by their Wyches – beneath the smile there is a smirk of anticipation, and concealed within the hand is a killing blade.

OBSESSION: ONLY THE STRONG WILL THRIVE

There is no place for frailty amongst the Cult of the Cursed Blade, for they teach that weakness exists only to be exploited by the strong. Those Wyches who survive in the Cult's arena are the physical embodiment of this philosophy.

- Add 1 to the Strength characteristic of models with this Obsession.
- Each time you make an unmodified saving throw of 6 for a model with this Obsession against a melee attack, after the attacking model's unit has finished making its attacks, that enemy unit suffers 1 mortal wound.

WARLORD TRAIT: TREACHEROUS DECEIVER

The Succubi of the Cult of the Cursed Blade are cunning and treacherous, exploiting any opportunity to wrong-foot and deceive their foes before striking them with concealed weapons.

Each time you make an unmodified saving throw of 4+ for this **WARLORD** against a melee attack, after the attacking model's unit has finished making its attacks, that enemy unit suffers 1 mortal wound. This **WARLORD** does not benefit from the second part of the Cursed Blades' Only the Strong Will Thrive Obsession.

RELIC: TRAITOR'S EMBRACE

The Traitor's Embrace comprises a pair of metal rods that are sewn into the skin. At the moment of death, these rods cause their bearer's bones to explode outward, rapidly growing into a jagged cage.

CULT OF THE CURSED BLADE SUCCUBUS model only. If the bearer is destroyed by a melee attack, roll one D6: on a 2+, after the attacking model's unit has finished making its attacks, it suffers D3+3 mortal wounds.

VENOMOUS SHARDBOMBS	1CP

Cult of the Cursed Blade – Wargear Stratagem

After luring their enemies towards them, the Cult of the Cursed Blade cast a volley of translucent charges into their midst that riddle the attackers with splinters of venomous shrapnel.

Use this Stratagem after the enemy has declared a charge against a **CULT OF THE CURSED BLADE WYCHES** unit from your army. That unit can fire Overwatch before the charge roll is made. When it does so, up to five models in that unit that are equipped with plasma grenades can make attacks with them, and until the end of the phase, plasma grenades this unit is equipped with gain the Poisoned Weapon (2+) ability.

WYCH CULTS

BATTLE-FORGED RULES

CULT OF THE RED GRIEF

*With acrobatic expertise and attacks so swift that few see them
coming, the Cult of the Red Grief revel in their capacity to slay
on the move, never stopping until all is bloody ruin. They strike,
kill and move on in the space a few desperate breaths, taking to
extremes the philosophy that the greatest defence is simply not to
be there when the opponent's blade falls.*

OBSESSION: THE SPEED OF THE KILL

*Wyches of the Cult of the Red Grief revel in high-speed murder,
and there is fierce competition amongst their ranks as to who can
butcher their victims the quickest.*

- You can re-roll charge rolls made for units with
  this Obsession.
- Add 2 to Advance rolls made for units with this Obsession.

WARLORD TRAIT: HYPERSWIFT REFLEXES

*The Succubi of the Cult of the Red Grief believe the best defence
is simply not to be there when the opponent's blade falls. Such are
their reflexes that they dodge blows with supernatural speed.*

Each time a melee attack is made against this **WARLORD**, an
unmodified hit roll of 1-3 for that attack fails, irrespective of
any abilities that the weapon or the model making the attack
may have.

RELIC: THE BLOOD GLAIVE

*Forged by Organghast the Haemomancer, the Blood Glaive
absorbs the viscera of those victims it slays. Sloughing off parts of
its blade that have become nicked in battle, the freshly harvested
gore is used to rehone its crimson edge.*

CULT OF THE RED GRIEF SUCCUBUS model equipped with an archite
glaive only. This Relic replaces an archite glaive and has the
following profile:

WEAPON	RANGE	TYPE	S	AP	D
The Blood Glaive	Melee	Melee	+2	-3	3

ATHLETIC AERIALISTS   1CP

Cult of the Red Grief – Strategic Ploy Stratagem

*Wyches of the Red Grief set foot on solid ground only for as long
as it takes to butcher the enemy.*

Use this Stratagem after a **CULT OF THE RED GRIEF INFANTRY** unit
has resolved its close combat attacks, but before it makes a
consolidation move. Instead of consolidating as normal, if every
model from this unit is within 6" of a friendly **CULT OF THE RED
GRIEF TRANSPORT** unit, they can embark in that **TRANSPORT** as if it
were the Movement phase even if this unit has disembarked this
turn, provided it has enough transport capacity remaining to
embark the whole unit.

Jeda Lynx watched the carnage unfold. A sliver
of lukewarm joy tugged at her cold heart at
the sight, though her envy for those Hellions
fighting was eclipsing it. It was her turn next to
battle, to feel the roar of the crowd reverberate over
her skin, to see her opponents sliced apart by her
perfectly crafted web of monofilament death.

Had it not been for the gate at the head of her
launch tunnel, covered in inward-facing barbed
spikes, Lynx would be out there already, hellglaive
in hand. Instead, she hovered as close as she could,
feet already locked into her skyboard.

Lynx laughed as she watched Uless Vexx be
dissected, head to groin, as she flew straight
through a wire left by Veshtari Krael. The severed
parts of the Hellion's corpse and skyboard dropped
into the fathomless depths of the Pit. There were
but two left now – Krael and Nathra Wysp. When
Wysp took a swipe at Krael with her hellglaive,
Lynx primed herself, ready to head straight into
the fray, but Wysp missed by a hair's breadth.

'Too slow, Nathra,' Lynx gibed.

What happened next took Lynx by surprise.
Within seconds of avoiding Wysp's strike, Krael
was killed. At the exact moment of her death, when
she flew into the wire, the lines of the cuts formed
the runic inscription for illusion – in this case, the
illusion of Wysp's strength, exposing her weakness.

The crowd roared, and Vorrskul's gate opened.

OTHER CULTS

If your chosen Cult does not have an associated Cult Obsession above, you must instead create their Cult Obsession by selecting two of the Obsessions from the lists below. An All-consuming Obsession counts as two selections.

ACROBATIC DISPLAY

This Cult favours spectacular gymnastic displays. Its fighters are never still, springing from one foot to the other and flipping over the blows of their foe with ease.

Each time a unit with this Obsession consolidates or piles in, models in that unit can move horizontally through other models and terrain features (they cannot finish a move on top of another model, or its base).

THE ART OF PAIN

Some Wych Cults elevate gladiatorial battles to another level by creating a spectacle that maims and cripples in order to draw out the moment of the kill, heightening the pleasure they derive before the final blade falls.

While a unit with this Obsession that has the Power From Pain ability is within Engagement Range of any enemy units, treat the current battle round number as being one higher when determining what effects the Power From Pain ability has.

BERSERK FUGUE (ALL-CONSUMING)

This Cult's warriors enter a killing trance when the moment of combat is joined, ripping their foes apart in a flurry of blows that owes nothing to grace and everything to bestial fury.

- Each time a model with this Obsession makes a melee attack, if that model's unit made a charge move, was charged or performed a Heroic Intervention this turn, an unmodified hit roll of 6 scores 1 additional hit.
- Each time a model with this Obsession would lose a wound as a result of a mortal wound, roll one D6: on a 5+, that wound is not lost.

PRECISE KILLERS

This Wych Cult is known for the meticulous skill of its warriors. Even the thickest armour is no defence against their assault, as blades plunge through eye lenses and slice through vulnerable seams.

Each time a model with this Obsession makes a melee attack, that attack benefits from the Blade Artists ability on an unmodified roll of 5+ instead of 6.

SLASHING IMPACT

The warriors of this Wych Cult are highly adept at using their bladed armour and equipment to plunge into the foe, opening up veins and slashing throats.

Each time a model with this Obsession finishes a charge move, you can select one enemy unit (excluding **VEHICLE** units) within Engagement Range and roll one D6: on a 6, that enemy unit suffers 1 mortal wound.

STIMULANT INNOVATORS

Not for this Cult the banal stimulants of their peers. Its fighters believe in trying ever-more interesting and dangerous concoctions to fuel their displays. From Ambull adrenal gland distillations to pheromonic infusions derived from the Ethereals of the T'au, these warriors will try anything to give themselves an edge over their opponents, the potential for metabolic meltdown only adding to the thrill.

Once per battle, in your Command phase, you can declare that units with this Obsession will use their experimental concoctions. When you do so, roll one D3 on the Combat Drugs table. Every unit with this Obsession that has the Combat Drugs ability gains this additional ability (which is cumulative with any abilities they already have) until the end of the turn.

TEST OF SKILL

This Wych Cult is driven to test its bladecraft against the largest and most dangerous foes in the galaxy. They are easily bored by slaughtering lesser opponents, but when faced with a truly monstrous quarry, they attack and dismember it with surprising speed and delight.

Each time a model with this Obsession makes a melee attack that targets a **MONSTER** or **VEHICLE** unit, add 1 to that attack's wound roll.

TROPHY TAKERS

Taking a token from each defeated foe, the members of this Cult are bedecked in patches of flayed skin, bones and skulls that proclaim their many victories.

Each time a Morale test is taken for an enemy unit that had any models destroyed by a melee attack made by a unit with this Obsession, roll one additional D6 and discard the lowest result.

AGILE HUNTERS (ALL-CONSUMING)

Training extensively among the haunted spires above their arenas, and renowned for dizzying extravaganzas that dangerously test their speed and reactions, these stimm-fuelled warriors are adept at chasing down the most elusive and mobile prey.

- Each time a model with this Obsession makes an attack that targets a unit that can **FLY**, add 1 to that attack's hit roll.
- If a unit with this Obsession with the Combat Drugs ability has the Hypex ability (pg 89), add 4" to that unit's Move characteristic instead of 3".

HAEMONCULUS COVENS

BATTLE-FORGED RULES

THE PROPHETS OF FLESH

No sadistic art is beyond the ken of these fleshcrafters and their countless, mutilated thralls.

OBSESSION: CONNOISSEURS OF PAIN

The Prophets of Flesh have modified their own bodies and those of their servants to an extraordinary extent – so much so that few weapons their enemies bring to bear against them can inflict damage greater than that they have already endured.

- At the start of your Command phase, each **Character**, **Grotesques** or **Monster** unit with this Obsession regains 1 lost wound.
- Each time an attack is made against a unit with this Obsession, unless that attack has a Strength characteristic of 8 or more, an unmodified wound roll of 1-3 for that attack fails, irrespective of any abilities that the weapon or the model making the attack may have.

WARLORD TRAIT: DIABOLICAL SOOTHSAYER

Many Haemonculi of the Prophets of Flesh dabble in soothsaying. The insights they gain by doing so allow them to modify their own bodies in preparation, either to foil a foreseen blow or to ensure the death of one who fate sought to spare.

When this model is set up on the battlefield, choose one of the below:

- Until the end of the battle, add 1 to this **Warlord**'s Toughness and Wounds characteristics.
- Until the end of the battle, add 1 to this **Warlord**'s Movement and Attacks characteristics.

RELIC: THE VEXATOR MASK

Fashioned from the flayed face of a Shadowseer, this mask plays tricks on the mind. The moment of hesitation this affords is enough for the wearer to plunge a surgical blade into the gawping viewer's heart.

Prophets of Flesh Haemonculus model only.

- Enemy units cannot fire Overwatch at the bearer.
- At the start of the Fight phase, you can select one enemy unit within 3" of the bearer. That unit is not eligible to fight this phase until after all eligible units from your army have done so.

SINS WRIT LARGE   1CP/2CP

Prophets of Flesh – Battle Tactic Stratagem

The Prophets of Flesh have innumerable servants, each of which is extensively marked with sigils of ownership by their masters. Only by committing the most impressive acts of sadism under the eyes of their betters can one of these twisted creatures slowly excise these marks.

Use this Stratagem at the start of the Fight phase. Select one **Prophets of Flesh Infantry** unit from your army that is within 6" of a friendly **Prophets of Flesh Haemonculus** unit. Until the end of the phase, each time an attack is made by this **Prophets of Flesh Infantry** unit you can re-roll the hit roll. If the selected unit is a **Grotesques** unit, this Stratagem costs 2CP; otherwise, it costs 1CP.

THE DARK CREED

Breaking the enemy's spirits is but the opening salvo for the members of the Dark Creed.

OBSESSION: DISTILLERS OF FEAR

The Coven of the Dark Creed has perfected every method of inducing fear, and their mere presence fills the mind with nightmarish dread.

Units with this Obsession have the following abilities:

- **Aura of Terror (Aura):** While an enemy unit is within 6" of a unit with this Obsession, subtract 1 from the Leadership characteristic of models in that unit, and subtract 1 from Combat Attrition tests made for that unit.
- Each time you make a melee attack for a unit with this Obsession that targets a unit with a Leadership characteristic that is equal to or lower than the attacking unit's Leadership characteristic, add 1 to that attack's hit roll.

WARLORD TRAIT: FEAR INCARNATE

The twisted Haemonculi of the Dark Creed have orchestrated the terror of others for so long that they exude an insanity-inducing aura. The sight of them is enough to drive their foes into such depths of despair that their hearts stop beating.

At the end of your Movement phase, you can select one enemy unit within 9" of this **WARLORD** and roll 3D6: if the result is greater than the enemy unit's Leadership characteristic, until the start of your next Movement phase, that enemy unit cannot perform actions (if that unit is currently performing an action, it immediately fails), and it loses the Objective Secured ability.

RELIC: SPIRIT-STING

The needles fired by Spirit-sting are loaded with dew collected from a sconce at the bottom of the Chasm of Echoes. When injected, it causes the victim's fears to manifest physically, bursting from their brain.

DARK CREED HAEMONCULUS model equipped with a stinger pistol only. This Relic replaces a stinger pistol and has the following profile:

WEAPON	RANGE	TYPE	S	AP	D
Spirit-sting	12"	Pistol 3	2	-3	1

Abilities: Poisoned Weapon (2+) (pg 89). Each time an attack is made with this weapon, invulnerable saving throws cannot be taken against that attack.

AN ESOTERIC KILL, DELIVERED FROM AFAR 2CP/3CP

The Dark Creed – Battle Tactic Stratagem

The Coven of the Dark Creed have a well-earned reputation for novel methods of assassination

Use this Stratagem when you select a **DARK CREED CORE** or **DARK CREED CHARACTER** unit from your army to shoot with. Until the end of the phase, each time you select a target for an attack made by this unit, you can ignore the Look Out, Sir rule. If the selected unit is a **TALOS** unit, this Stratagem costs 3CP; otherwise, it costs 2CP.

THE COVEN OF TWELVE

Gruesome masters of up-close butchery, the Coven of Twelve engage in escalating acts of inventive misery and violence.

OBSESSION: BUTCHERS OF FLESH

The practice of internecine assassinations that exists amongst the Coven of Twelve ensures that weapons and wits are kept razor-sharp at all times, and only those members who exist in a state of hyperawareness – keeping a meticulously honed blade nearby at all times – survive long.

- Each time a model with this Obsession makes an attack with a melee weapon (excluding Relics), improve the Armour Penetration characteristic of that attack by 1.
- If a unit with this Obsession is performing an action, it can still make attacks with ranged weapons without that action failing.

WARLORD TRAIT: SCARLET EPICUREAN

The Haemonculi of the Coven of Twelve have been slain and resurrected so many times that there are few methods of death they are not intimately familiar with. Unless they wish to experience a new fatality, they are notoriously difficult to kill.

Each time an attack is allocated to this **WARLORD**, subtract 1 from the Damage characteristic of that attack (to a minimum of 1).

RELIC: THE FLENSING BLADE

This blade allows its wielder to expertly carve samples of skin, fat and musculature from their victims for experimentation.

COVEN OF TWELVE HAEMONCULUS model equipped with Haemonculus tools only. This Relic replaces Haemonculus tools and has the following profile:

WEAPON	RANGE	TYPE	S	AP	D
The Flensing Blade	Melee	Melee	User	-2	D3

Abilities: Poisoned Weapon (2+) (pg 89). Each time an attack made with this weapon targets a **CHARACTER** unit, that attack has a Damage characteristic of 3.

A MOST INVENTIVE DEMISE   1CP

Coven of Twelve – Epic Deed Stratagem

Amidst the treacherous Coven of Twelve, the art of assassination is held in high regard, with the most unique and inventive techniques garnering significant prestige. Many Haemonculi have been removed from this esteemed conclave, using methods perfected on the battlefield by their rivals.

Use this Stratagem after a **COVEN OF TWELVE HAEMONCULUS** unit from your army consolidates. Select one enemy **CHARACTER** model (excluding **VEHICLE** or **MONSTER** models) that is within Engagement Range of this **HAEMONCULUS** unit and roll one D6. On a 2-5 that model suffers D3 mortal wounds. On a 6 that model suffers D3+3 mortal wounds.

OTHER COVENS

If your chosen Coven does not have an associated Coven Obsession, you must instead create their Coven Obsession by selecting two of the Obsessions from the lists below. An All-consuming Obsession counts as two selections.

ARTISTS OF THE FLESH (ALL-CONSUMING)
The surgeon-artisans of this Coven are true masters of their craft. The sickening products of depraved laboratories, they emerge tougher and more resilient than their rivals.

Each time an attack is allocated to a model with this Obsession (excluding **Vehicle** models), subtract 1 from the Damage characteristic of that attack (to a minimum of 1).

DARK HARVEST
This Coven waits with the patience of a spider before descending on its victims in great force to gather a harvest of terror and flesh.

Each time a unit with this Obsession finishes a charge move, you can select one enemy unit (excluding **Vehicle** units) within Engagement Range and roll one D6: on a 4+, that enemy unit suffers 1 mortal wound.

DARK TECHNOMANCERS (ALL-CONSUMING)
The products of this Coven are highly sought after, their baleful technologies drawing upon the more unstable and destructive energies of the galaxy. Judged alongside such gloriously potent carnage, Haemonculi care little about the risk to their own thralls.

Each time a unit with this Obsession is selected to shoot, you can choose to enhance any or all of the ranged weapons models in that unit are equipped with. If you do so, until the end of the phase, each time an attack is made with an enhanced weapon, add 1 to that attack's wound roll and add 1 to the Damage characteristic of that attack, but that attack's hit roll cannot be re-rolled. If any unmodified hit rolls of 1 are made for attacks with an enhanced weapon, the bearer's unit suffers 1 mortal wound after shooting with this weapon. If the bearer is a **Vehicle** or **Monster** model, it suffers D3 mortal wounds instead.

EXPERIMENTAL CREATIONS
To a greater extent than other Haemonculi, the rulers of this Coven repeatedly experiment on their followers and even themselves. Test subjects are often intravenously fed varieties of strength-enhancing concoctions with which to tear into the enemy – to the delight of their masters.

Add 1 to the Strength characteristic of models with this Obsession.

HUNGRY FOR FLESH
The Haemonculi of this Coven are consumed with the need to sate their appetite for fresh flesh – either to gorge themselves or experiment upon it, according to each individual's whim.

You can re-roll charge rolls made for units with this Obsession.

MASTERS OF MUTAGENS
Fascination with the fragility of their foes' genetic structures drives this Coven. Crafting horrific poisons, the Haemonculi put these to spectacular use on the battlefield, the most innocuous wound leading to rapid and explosive mutations.

Each time a model with this Obsession makes a melee attack with a poisoned weapon (excluding Relics) that targets a unit that is not a **Vehicle** or **Titanic**, an unmodified hit roll of 6 automatically wounds the target.

MASTER TORTURERS
The flensing caress and needle-fingered grip of these sadistic monsters finds every pain receptor and hidden weakness of their luckless victims.

Each time a unit with this Obsession is selected for the Torturer's Craft Stratagem (pg 68), reduce the Command point cost of that Stratagem by 1.

OBSESSIVE COLLECTORS
The members of this Coven compulsively collect samples of all the many races of the galaxy. Their followers absorb fluids and other substances from their defeated foes, invigorating their own ravaged forms.

Each time an enemy unit is destroyed by a melee attack made by a unit with this Obsession, a model in that attacking unit can regain D3 lost wounds. Each model can only be healed once per turn. If the attacking unit is a **Wrack** unit, D3 destroyed models can be added back to the unit. These models can only be set up within Engagement Range of enemy units that are already within Engagement Range of this unit and no longer count as having been destroyed for the purposes of Morale tests this turn.

ENHANCED SENSORY ORGANS
This Coven have replaced their sensoria with knotted bundles of fleshy ganglia. Unhindered even by their thralls' impassive masks, the arcane perception they grant ensures no prey can hide from them.

Each time a model with this Obsession makes an attack, the target does not receive the benefits of Light Cover or Heavy Cover against that attack.

SPLINTERBLADES
Each cut made by a member of this Coven leaves a series of vibrating shards in the victim's flesh, agitating the skin around the wound and ensuring their foe bleeds out all the faster.

Each time a model with this Obsession makes an attack with a melee weapon, an unmodified hit roll of 6 scores 1 additional hit.

EXAMPLE: REALSPACE RAID

This example shows Alex's Strike-Force-sized Drukhari army organised into a single Battalion Detachment. Alex has designated this Detachment as a Realspace Raid Detachment (pg 49).

Alex's army includes an **ARCHON** unit (the **WARLORD**) from the Kabal of the Black Heart, a **MASTER SUCCUBUS** unit from the Cult of the Cursed Blade and a **HAEMONCULUS** unit from The Hex. Because this Detachment is a Realspace Raid Detachment – and contains the required units as described on page 49 – every **KABAL OF THE BLACK HEART** unit in that Detachment gains the Thirst for Power Obsession, and every **CULT OF THE CURSED BLADE** unit in that Detachment gains the Only the Strong Will Thrive Obsession. Because The Hex are not one of the Haemonculus Covens listed on pages 62-64, Alex must instead create a Coven Obsession for them from the ones listed on page 65. Alex chooses the Experimental Creations and Splinterblades Obsessions. Because this Detachment is a Realspace Raid Detachment, every **THE HEX** unit in that Detachment gains these chosen Obsessions.

Because Alex has made the **ARCHON** unit the **WARLORD**, it can be given the Kabal of the Black Heart's Labyrinthine Cunning Warlord Trait. Alex has also spent 1 Command point to use the Alliance of Agony Stratagem. Because of this, the **MASTER SUCCUBUS** unit has been given the Cult of the Cursed Blade's Treacherous Deceiver Warlord Trait (pg 59), and the **HAEMONCULUS** unit has been given the Master Nemesine Warlord Trait (pg 73).

Alex has designated this Detachment as a Realspace Raid, so Command points can be spent during the battle to use the Agents of Vect Stratagem because the **WARLORD** is from the Kabal of the Black Heart. As the Detachment includes a **MASTER SUCCUBUS** unit from the Cult of the Cursed Blade, Alex can also use the Venomous Shardbombs Stratagem in addition to those found on pages 68-70, and any that can be used from other publications (such as the Core Stratagems in the Warhammer 40,000 Core Book).

Because this Detachment is a Realspace Raid, Alex has given the **MASTER SUCCUBUS** unit the Cult of the Cursed Blade's Relic (instead of only being able to select the Writ of the Living Muse because a **KABAL OF THE BLACK HEART** model is the **WARLORD**, or one of the Artefacts of Cruelty listed on pages 74-75). However, Alex has also spent 2 Command points to use the Prizes from the Dark City Stratagem twice, allowing Alex to give the **ARCHON** unit the Writ of the Living Muse Relic, and give the **HAEMONCULUS** unit the Animus Vitae from the Artefacts of Cruelty.

HQ

- Archon
- Succubus upgraded with Show Stealer Wych Cult Spectacle
- Haemonculus

TROOPS

- 2 Units of 10 Kabalite Warriors
- 1 Unit of 10 Wyches upgraded to be Hekatrix Bloodbrides
- 1 Unit of 15 Wracks

ELITES

- 10 Incubi

FAST ATTACK

- 6 Reavers
- 5 Hellions
- 5 Scourges

HEAVY SUPPORT

- 3 Talos

DEDICATED TRANSPORTS

- 3 Raiders

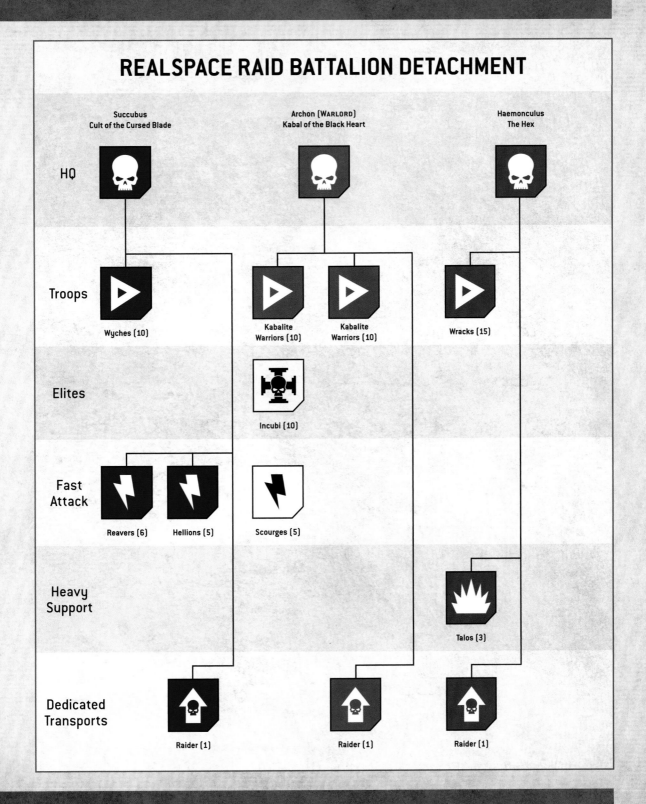

REALSPACE RAID BATTALION DETACHMENT

Succubus
Cult of the Cursed Blade

Archon (WARLORD)
Kabal of the Black Heart

Haemonculus
The Hex

HQ

Troops

Wyches (10)

Kabalite
Warriors (10)

Kabalite
Warriors (10)

Wracks (15)

Elites

Incubi (10)

**Fast
Attack**

Reavers (6)

Hellions (5)

Scourges (5)

**Heavy
Support**

Talos (3)

**Dedicated
Transports**

Raider (1)

Raider (1)

Raider (1)

STRATAGEMS

If your army includes any **DRUKHARI** Detachments (excluding Auxiliary Support, Super-heavy Auxiliary or Fortification Network Detachments), you have access to these Stratagems, and can spend CPs to use them.

CRUEL DECEPTION   1CP/2CP

Drukhari – Battle Tactic Stratagem

Commorrite society is founded upon opportunistic deception.

Use this Stratagem in your Movement phase, when a **DRUKHARI** unit from your army Falls Back. You can select for this unit to be eligible to shoot this turn or eligible to declare a charge this turn, or both. If you select both, this Stratagem costs 2CP; otherwise, it costs 1CP.

THE GREAT ENEMY   1CP

Drukhari – Battle Tactic Stratagem

The Chaos God Slaanesh is reviled by the Aeldari, who hate and despise his followers with a ferocious loathing.

Use this Stratagem in the Fight phase, when a **DRUKHARI** unit from your army is selected to fight. Until the end of the phase, each time a model in that unit makes a melee attack against a **SLAANESH** unit, you can re-roll the hit roll and you can re-roll wound roll.

THE TORTURER'S CRAFT   1CP/2CP

Drukhari – Battle Tactic Stratagem

Over long millennia in Commorragh's undercity, the Haemonculus Covens have perfected the craft of carving flesh.

Use this Stratagem in the Fight phase when **URIEN RAKARTH** or a **<HAEMONCULUS COVEN>** unit from your army is selected to fight. Until the end of the phase, each time a model in that unit makes an attack, you can re-roll the wound roll. If this Stratagem is used when a **CHARACTER** or **WRACKS** unit that contains 10 or less models is selected to fight, it costs 1CP; otherwise, it costs 2CP.

LIGHTNING FAST REACTIONS   1CP

Drukhari – Battle Tactic Stratagem

The hyper-fast reflexes of the Drukhari allow them to duck and weave to avoid all but the swiftest enemy strikes.

Use this Stratagem in your opponent's Shooting phase or the Fight phase, when a **DRUKHARI INFANTRY**, **DRUKHARI VEHICLE** or **DRUKHARI BIKER** unit from your army (excluding **URIEN RAKARTH** or a **<HAEMONCULUS COVEN>** unit) is selected as the target of an attack. Until the end of the phase, each time an attack is made against that unit, subtract 1 from that attack's hit roll.

HUNT FROM THE SHADOWS   1CP

Drukhari – Battle Tactic Stratagem

The denizens of Commorragh use the shadows to their advantage.

Use this Stratagem in your opponent's Shooting phase, when a **DRUKHARI** unit from your army that has the benefits of Light Cover is selected as the target of a ranged attack. Until the end of that phase, add an additional 1 to that unit's saving throws (excluding invulnerable saving throws).

ALLIANCE OF AGONY   1CP

Drukhari – Requisition Stratagem

Even the most bloodthirsty Drukhari will veil their enmity to work together against a shared enemy for the same gruesome purpose.

Use this Stratagem before the battle, when you are mustering your army, if your **WARLORD** is a **REALSPACE RAIDER ARCHON**. Select one **SUCCUBUS** model from your army and one **HAEMONCULUS** model from your army (excluding named characters) and determine one Warlord Trait for each of these models (this must be a Warlord Trait it can have); those models are only regarded as your **WARLORD** for the purposes of that Warlord Trait. Each Warlord Trait in your army must be unique (if randomly generated, re-roll duplicate results), and you cannot use this Stratagem to give a model two Warlord Traits. You can only use this Stratagem once.

TOLERATED AMBITION   1CP

Drukhari – Requisition Stratagem

Confident leaders might delegate some duties to a monitored underling, one easily disposed of if need be…

Use this Stratagem before the battle, when you are mustering your army, if your **WARLORD** has the **DRUKHARI** keyword. Select one **DRUKHARI CHARACTER** model from your army (excluding named characters) and determine one Warlord Trait for it (this must be a Warlord Trait it can have); that model it is only regarded as your **WARLORD** for the purposes of that Warlord Trait. Each Warlord Trait in your army must be unique (if randomly generated, re-roll duplicate results), and you cannot use this Stratagem to give a model two Warlord Traits. You can only use this Stratagem once, unless you are playing a Strike Force battle (in which case, you can use this Stratagem twice) or an Onslaught battle (in which case, you can use this Stratagem three times).

PRIZES FROM THE DARK CITY   1CP

Drukhari – Requisition Stratagem

A warlord who wants their high status to be known will equip their raiding parties with the most extravagant weaponry.

Use this Stratagem before the battle, when you are mustering your army, if your **WARLORD** has the **DRUKHARI** keyword. Select one **DRUKHARI CHARACTER** model from your army and give them one Artefact of Cruelty (this must be a Relic they can have). Each Relic in your army must be unique, and you cannot use this Stratagem to give a model two Relics. You can only use this Stratagem once, unless you are playing a Strike Force battle (in which case, you can use this Stratagem twice) or an Onslaught battle (in which case, you can use this Stratagem three times).

WEBWAY PORTAL   1CP/3CP

Drukhari – Strategic Ploy Stratagem

By hurling rune-graven orbs into the air, the Drukhari can tear a route into the webway through which more of their kin can pour.

Use this Stratagem before the battle when declaring reserves and transports (if you are playing a mission without this step, use this Stratagem during deployment instead). If you spend 1CP, you can set up one **DRUKHARI INFANTRY**, **BIKER** or **BEAST** unit from your army in the webway instead of placing it on the battlefield. If you spend 3CPs, you can place two **DRUKHARI INFANTRY**, **BIKER** or **BEAST** units in the webway instead.

In the Reinforcements step of one of your Movement phases, you can set up any units in the webway anywhere on the battlefield that is more than 9" away from any enemy models. You can only use this Stratagem once.

PAIN SYPHON   1CP

Drukhari – Strategic Ploy Stratagem

Cronos parasite engines absorb and magnify the agonies of nearby foes, driving their fellow raiders into a frenzy.

Use this Stratagem when a **DRUKHARI** unit from your army that is within 6" of a friendly **CRONOS** unit destroys an enemy unit with a melee or ranged attack. Until the end of the battle, that **DRUKHARI** unit always treats each battle round as if it is battle round 5 for the purposes of the Power From Pain ability.

EVISCERATING FLY-BY   1CP/2CP

Drukhari – Strategic Ploy Stratagem

The airborne combatants of a Wych Cult have no need to slow down in order to carry out their slaughter.

Use this Stratagem in your Movement phase, when you select a **<WYCH CULT>** unit that can **FLY** to make a Normal Move or Advance. After this unit has moved, select one enemy unit this unit moved across and roll one D6 for each model in this unit, adding 1 to the result if the enemy unit is an **INFANTRY** unit: for each result of 5+, that enemy unit suffers 1 mortal wound. If the selected **<WYCH CULT>** unit contains 5 or fewer models, this Stratagem costs 1CP; otherwise, it costs 2CP.

NEVER STATIONARY   2CP

Drukhari – Strategic Ploy Stratagem

The Drukhari are masters at using hit-and-run tactics, engaging a target with a flurry of shots before quickly manoeuvring into cover or out of sight.

Use this Stratagem in your Shooting phase after making attacks with a **DRUKHARI** unit (excluding **AIRCRAFT** units) from your army. That unit can immediately make a Normal Move of up to 7". Until the end of the turn, that unit is not eligible to declare a charge.

PREY ON THE WEAK   1CP

Drukhari – Strategic Ploy Stratagem

The scent of a foe in pain draws Drukhari to it like hungry predators to an injured beast, their senses sharpening at its tang.

Use this Stratagem in your Shooting phase or the Fight phase, when a **DRUKHARI CORE** unit from your army is selected to shoot or fight. Until the end of the phase, each time a model in this unit makes an attack:

- If that attack targets a unit that was below its starting strength when this unit was selected to shoot or fight, re-roll a hit roll of 1.
- If that attack targets a unit that was below Half-strength when this unit was selected to shoot or fight, you can re-roll the hit roll.

SCREAMING JETS   1CP

Drukhari – Strategic Ploy Stratagem

Just as terrifying as a sudden emergence from the webway is the meteoric descent of a Drukhari raiding craft behind enemy lines.

Use this Stratagem before the battle when declaring reserves and transports (if you are playing a mission without this step, use this Stratagem during deployment instead). You can set up one **DRUKHARI VEHICLE** unit from your army in the skies instead of placing it on the battlefield.

In the Reinforcements step of one of your Movement phases, you can set up this unit anywhere on the battlefield that is more than 9" away from any enemy models. You can only use this Stratagem once.

DEADLY RIVALS   2CP

Drukhari – Strategic Ploy Stratagem

Hellions and Reavers frequently spar for prestige and dominance, both in the arenas and high above the bloody streets of the Dark City.

Use this Stratagem in your Command phase. Select one **REAVERS** unit from your army and one **HELLIONS** unit from your army that are within 12" of and visible to each other. Until the end of the turn:

- Add 1" to the Movement characteristics of models in these units.
- Each time a model in these units makes an attack with a melee weapon, you can re-roll the hit roll.

SWIFT OUTFLANKING — 1CP

Drukhari – Strategic Ploy Stratagem

Transport barques seek to ferry their murderous cargo on new attack angles, or else move aloft to provide encircling fire support.

Use this Stratagem at the end of your Movement phase. Select one **Drukhari Transport** unit from your army that is wholly within 9" of any battlefield edge. Remove that unit from the battlefield. That unit is placed into Strategic Reserves.

MURDEROUS DESCENT — 1CP

Drukhari – Strategic Ploy Stratagem

As their transports descend, Drukhari are swift to plunge into their prey, blades bared.

Use this Stratagem in the Reinforcements step, after a **Transport** unit from your army is set up on the battlefield. Any units embarked upon that **Transport** unit can disembark after it is set up, but when they do so, they must be set up more than 9" away from any enemy units.

PRAY THEY DON'T TAKE YOU ALIVE — 1CP

Drukhari – Epic Deed Stratagem

Few armies are able to maintain their mettle when the sounds of their leader's tortured screams fill the air.

Use this Stratagem in the Fight phase, when an enemy **Warlord** unit is destroyed by a melee attack made by a **Drukhari** unit from your army. Until the end of the battle, each time a Combat Attrition test is taken for an enemy unit, subtract 1 from that Combat Attrition test.

ENHANCED AETHERSAILS — 1CP

Drukhari – Wargear Stratagem

Drukhari raiding craft bear many enhancements that allow for lightning-fast attacks and swift withdrawals.

Use this Stratagem in your Movement phase, when a **Raider** or **Ravager** unit from your army is selected to Advance. Do not make an Advance roll. Instead, until the end of the phase, add 8" to the Move characteristic of this model.

CRUCIBLE OF MALEDICTION — 2CP

Drukhari – Wargear Stratagem

When opened, the souls of tortured psykers spew outward, driving insane any nearby whose minds are attuned to the warp.

Use this Stratagem in your Psychic phase. Select one **Haemonculus** unit from your army and roll one D6 for each enemy **Psyker** unit within 12" of it; for each roll of 4+, that **Psyker** unit suffers D3 mortal wounds. You can only use this Stratagem once.

HAYWIRE GRENADE — 1CP

Drukhari – Wargear Stratagem

Haywire grenades send out a powerful electromagnetic pulse to debilitate and damage enemy vehicles.

Use this Stratagem in your Shooting phase, when a **Drukhari Haywire Grenade** unit from your army is selected to shoot. Select one model in that unit; that model can only make one attack this phase, and must target an enemy **Vehicle** unit within 6" of it, but if a hit is scored, that **Vehicle** unit suffers D3 mortal wounds and the attack sequence ends.

HYPERSTIMM BACKLASH — 2CP

Drukhari – Wargear Stratagem

Heedless of the brutal effects of overdosing, members of a Wych Cult may take a massive dose of combat drugs to further enhance their combat prowess.

Use this Stratagem in your Command phase. Select one **<Wych Cult>** unit with the Combat Drugs ability from your army. Until your next Command phase, each effect of the Combat Drugs ability on that unit is doubled (e.g. if the unit is affected by Painbringer, add 2 to the Toughness characteristic of models affected by that combat drug instead of 1). A model with the Phial Bouquet Relic cannot be selected for this Stratagem.

SHOCK PROW — 1CP

Drukhari – Wargear Stratagem

Many Drukhari outfit their vehicles with energised rams which, when activated, emit directional waves of force, capable of carving through infantry formations and even shattering the hulls of tanks.

Use this Stratagem in the Charge phase, when a **Drukhari Shock Prow** unit from your army finishes a charge move. Select one enemy unit within Engagement Range of that **Shock Prow** unit:
- If the selected enemy unit is a **Vehicle** unit, roll one D6: on a 2+, that unit suffers D3 mortal wounds.
- If the selected enemy unit is not a **Vehicle** unit, roll one D6 for each model in that enemy unit that is within Engagement Range of the **Shock Prow** unit. For each dice result that equals or exceeds that enemy unit's Toughness characteristic, it suffers 1 mortal wound.

POTENT METALLOTOXINS — 2CP

Drukhari – Wargear Stratagem

A few rare poisons contain virulent acidic compounds, ferrogangrenous venoms or even inorganic nanophages, which swiftly break down the most formidable of armour plating. When showered with these potent shards, enemy crews find their vehicles dissolving around them, or even swelling with infection and crushing them inside.

Use this Stratagem in your Shooting phase or the Fight phase, when you select a **Drukhari** unit from your army to shoot or fight. Until the end of the phase, each time an attack is made with a poisoned weapon (pg 89) (excluding Relics) by that unit, that ability does not exclude **Vehicle** units (though it does still exclude **Titanic** units).

70

CHAPTER APPROVED RULES

If every model in your army (excluding **Unaligned** models) has the **Drukhari** keyword, and your **Warlord** has the **Drukhari** keyword, you can, if you are playing a matched play battle that instructs you to select secondary objectives (e.g. a mission from the Eternal War mission pack in the Warhammer 40,000 Core Book), select one of them to be from the **Drukhari** secondary objectives listed below.

Like all other secondary objectives, each of the secondary objectives listed below has a category, and they follow all the normal rules for secondary objectives (for example, when you select secondary objectives, you cannot choose more than one from each category, you can score no more than 15 victory points from each secondary objective you select during the mission etc.).

PURGE THE ENEMY

TAKE THEM ALIVE!

Progressive Objective

The Drukhari raid the galaxy's worlds with a single aim uppermost in their minds: the capture of living beings. Once violently subdued and secured with all manner of tortuous bindings, these unfortunate souls are taken back to the Dark City where a horrible fate awaits them. Whether as bait in the arenas, fresh meat upon a filthy, surgical slab or a bruised plaything for their new masters, the victim's existence now has only one purpose – their agonies and sorrow are fodder to invigorate and nourish their captors.

If you select this objective, you score victory points at the end of the battle for each of the following that apply:

- Score 3 victory points if any **Character** or **Monster** units were destroyed by a melee attack made by a **Drukhari** unit from your army during that battle round.

- Score 1 victory point if any unit (excluding **Character**, **Monster** or **Vehicle** units) were destroyed by a melee attack made by a **Drukhari** unit from your army during that battle round.

BEASTS FOR THE ARENAS

End Game Objective

Many of these vicious beasts will not last a single show of bloodletting. Those with enough savagery for that may not endure the cruel attentions of the Beastmasters. Yet for those feral and exotic monstrosities that leave the audiences roaring for more… for one of those, a Wych could name their price.

Score 3 victory points at the end of the battle for each enemy **Monster**, **Cavalry** or **Beast** unit that was destroyed by a melee attack made by a <**Wych Cult**> unit from your army. If that enemy unit was **Titanic**, score 5 victory points for it instead.

NO MERCY, NO RESPITE

FEAR AND TERROR

Progressive Objective

Sowing terror in the foe's ranks and sending them fleeing is of great physical and strategic value to the Drukhari. Alongside pain and anguish, it feeds their withered souls, granting them a form of supernatural vigour. Fear is infectious, spreading through the remaining enemy force, softening them up for the Drukhari's final, swift assault. Those who run furthest will provide diverting hunting sport at battle's end, a gift from the raid's leader to their followers. Some will even be spared, alive yet scarred inside and out, to gibber of nightmares and changelings for years to come. Their warnings will degenerate into horrifying fairy tales of stolen children and hooks, poisonous beauty and cruel laughter that gnaws at the society's consciousness, preparing them subtly for the next raid in a century – or decade's – time. Yet, were none of that true, the Drukhari would still terrify, torture and flense their foes for one, simple reason. They like doing it.

Score 1 victory point at the end of the battle round for each model that fled from any enemy unit during that battle round.

BATTLEFIELD SUPREMACY

HERD THE PREY

Progressive Objective

The Drukhari rarely linger during realspace raids, as the efficient corralling of their inevitable prey is of great import. Protracted meat grinders do not suit their style of warfare, and they avoid – where possible – the enemy's lumbering reinforcements. Their swift-moving raiding forces often seek to encircle and drive the foe together so there can be no escape, clustering their enemies like bewildered grox awaiting shipment to the abattoir.

Score 2 victory points at the end of your turn for each table quarter that does not have any enemy units (excluding **Aircraft** units) wholly within it. This objective cannot be scored in the first battle round.

WARLORD TRAITS

If a **DRUKHARI CHARACTER** model is your **WARLORD**, you can use the Drukhari Warlord Traits tables opposite to determine what Warlord Trait they have. Unless otherwise specified, **<KABAL>** models must use the Kabal Warlord Traits table, **<WYCH CULT>** models must use the Wych Cults Warlord Traits table and **<HAEMONCULUS COVEN>** models must use the Haemonculus Covens Warlord Traits table. You can either roll one D3 to randomly generate one, or you can select one.

When you have determined a Warlord Trait for a **DRUKHARI CHARACTER** model, replace all instances of the **<KABAL>**, **<WYCH CULT>** or **<HAEMONCULUS COVEN>** keyword in their Warlord Trait (if any) with the name of the Kabal, Wych Cult or Haemonculus Coven that your model is drawn from.

NAMED CHARACTERS AND WARLORD TRAITS

If one of the following characters gains a Warlord Trait, they must have the one shown below:

Named Character	Warlord Trait
Drazhar	Hatred Eternal
Lelith Hesperax	Blood Dancer (pg 58)
Urien Rakarth	Diabolical Soothsayer (pg 62)

KABAL WARLORD TRAITS

1. HATRED ETERNAL
This warlord is disgusted by the younger races that infest the galaxy, sickened by the unwashed and unrefined multitudes. They will take any opportunity to exterminate such vermin.

Each time this **WARLORD** makes an attack, you can re-roll the hit roll and the wound roll.

2. SOUL THIRST
In place of a soul, this warlord plays host to a howling chasm of horror and madness. They must swallow thousands of souls each day to stave off complete degeneration, yet this thirst lends them a lethal ferocity.

- Add 1 to the Attacks characteristic of this **WARLORD**.
- Once per turn, when an enemy model that is within 6" of this **WARLORD** is destroyed, this model regains 1 lost wound.

3. ANCIENT EVIL
So long has this warlord lived, steeped in horror and cruelty, that their very gaze is said to be capable of paralysing their foes with fear.

At the start of the Fight phase, you can select one enemy unit within Engagement Range of this **WARLORD**. That unit is not eligible to fight this phase until after all eligible units from your army have done so.

WYCH CULT WARLORD TRAITS

1. QUICKSILVER FIGHTER
This warlord strikes with preternatural speed, slaying their foes before they even realise the fight has begun.

Add 2 to the Attacks characteristic of this **WARLORD**.

2. STIMM ADDICT
Though it entails all manner of horrific side effects, this warlord is addicted to using artificial stimulants to boost their combat effectiveness.

When determining the effects of the Combat Drugs ability for this **WARLORD** before the battle, roll 2 additional dice, re-rolling results of 6 or results that are already in effect. This **WARLORD**'s Combat Drugs ability has these benefits in addition to any others.

3. PRECISION BLOWS
This warlord is adept at slaying in a stunning display of violence, every blow placed perfectly to dismember or decapitate.

Each time an unmodified hit roll of 6 is made for a melee attack made by this **WARLORD**, the target unit suffers a number of mortal wounds equal to the Damage characteristic of the weapon used for that attack, and the attack sequence ends.

HAEMONCULUS COVEN WARLORD TRAITS

1. MASTER REGENESIST
A master of fleshcrafting, this creature can rejuvenate even the most seriously wounded of minions with a flick of their bladed fingers.

Each time this **WARLORD** uses their Fleshcraft ability, the target model regains up to 3 lost wounds instead of D3.

2. MASTER NEMESINE
This warlord knows a variety of ways to kill every realspace species they have ever discovered. There is no weak point unknown to them.

Each time this **WARLORD** makes an attack, add 1 to that attack's wound roll.

3. MASTER ARTISAN
This warlord is not only gifted in the arts of fleshcrafting and mettalosculpture, but also in the more metaphysical arts. Irrespective of the medium they work with, it is their own twisted body that bears the greatest hallmarks of their dark genius.

Add 1 to the Toughness and Wounds characteristics of this **WARLORD**.

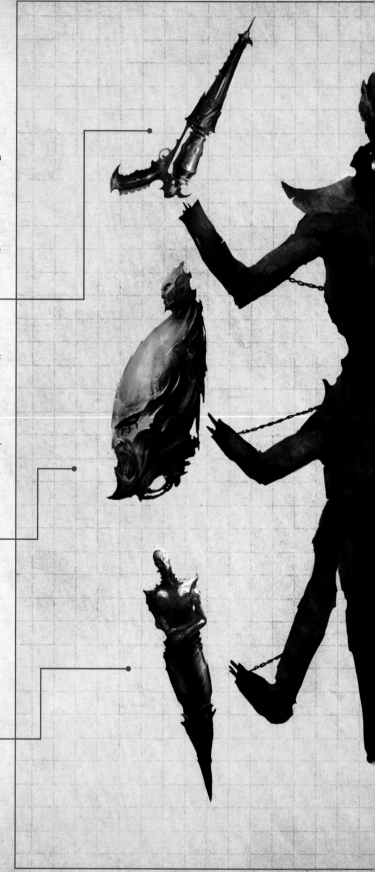

RELICS

If your army is led by a **DRUKHARI WARLORD**, you can, when mustering your army, give one of the following Artefacts of Cruelty to a **DRUKHARI CHARACTER** model in your army. Named characters cannot be given any of the following Relics.

When a model in your army is given an Artefact of Cruelty, replace all instances of the **<KABAL>**, **<WYCH CULT>** or **<HAEMONCULUS COVEN>** keyword in that Relic's rules (if any) with the name of the Kabal, Wych Cult or Haemonculus Coven that your model is drawn from.

Note that some Relics replace one of the model's existing items of wargear. Where this is the case, you must, if you are using points values, still pay the cost of the wargear that is being replaced. Write down any Artefacts of Cruelty your models have on your army roster.

PARASITE'S KISS

Thought to be the finest splinter pistol ever crafted, this weapon spits out crystalline darts bound with psycho-vampiric circuitry. Upon biting into their flesh, the target's very soul is leeched and transferred back to the gun's wielder. As the luckless victim withers like rotten fruit, their killer flushes with vigour.

Model equipped with a splinter pistol only. This Relic replaces a splinter pistol and has the following profile:

WEAPON	RANGE	TYPE	S	AP	D
Parasite's Kiss	12"	Pistol 3	2	-2	2

Abilities: Poisoned Weapon (2+) (pg 89). Each time an enemy model is destroyed by an attack made with this weapon, the bearer regains 1 lost wound.

THE HELM OF SPITE

The Drukhari look down upon those who use psychic witchery. Not only do they tempt the gaze of She Who Thirsts, but they also risk the wrath of Asdrubael Vect. Through necessity, the Drukhari's psychic abilities have atrophied, leaving them vulnerable to the warpcraft of their foes. The Helm of Spite redresses this imbalance, shielding its wearer from harm and setting up a field of violent psionic feedback.

In your opponent's Psychic phase, the bearer can attempt to deny one psychic power as if it were a **PSYKER**. If that psychic power is successfully denied, the **PSYKER** attempting to manifest that power suffers Perils of the Warp.

THE NIGHTMARE DOLL

Should the owner of the Nightmare Doll be harmed in battle, his injuries are absorbed by this creature. If its owner is riddled with bullets, tiny holes appear in the thing's writhing body whilst its master remains whole. Should the Haemonculus be hit by a decapitating strike, the foe's blade will pass through his gnarled neck without leaving so much as a scratch.

HAEMONCULUS model only. Each time the bearer would lose a wound, roll one D6: on a 4+, that wound is not lost.

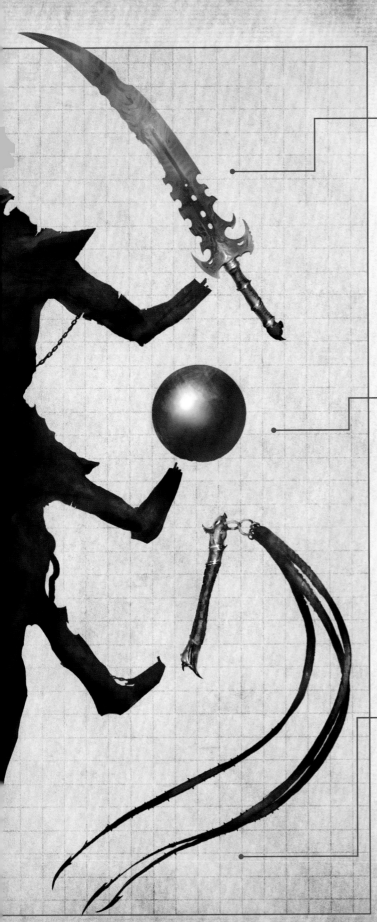

THE DJIN BLADE

Forged from an unknown alloy, the Djin Blade reflects an idealised reflection of whoever looks at it. Though the blade lends its wielder incredible prowess, it will feed off their essence until it turns upon them. On that day, the wielder's reflection shifts into something malefic, the true face of the Djin leering out at them before it turns their heart to ash and their soul to drifting cinders.

Model equipped with a huskblade only. This Relic replaces a huskblade and has the following profile:

WEAPON	RANGE	TYPE	S	AP	D
The Djin Blade	Melee	Melee	+1	-3	3

Abilities: Each time the bearer fights, it makes 2 additional attacks with this weapon. At the end of the Fight phase, roll one D6 if the bearer made any attacks with this weapon: on a 1, the bearer suffers 1 mortal wound.

THE ANIMUS VITAE

The Animus Vitae appears to be a smooth orb, until it is thrown at the feet of a victim and explodes into a lashing tangle of barbed wires that wrap around its prey. Slowly and spitefully, the Animus Vitae begins to constrict, cutting through armour, flesh and bone until its victim's agonised cries become desperate screams. All the while the foul weapon radiates this agony, saturating the battlefield with pain so that the bearer and his kin can drink it in like a potent draught.

The Animus Vitae has the following profile:

WEAPON	RANGE	TYPE	S	AP	D
The Animus Vitae	6"	Grenade 1	-	-	-

Abilities: The bearer can only shoot with this weapon once per battle. If it hits, the target unit suffers D3 mortal wounds. If the target unit has 11 or more models, it suffers D3+3 mortal wounds instead. Until the end of the turn, friendly units with the Power From Pain ability (pg 89) treat the current battle round as being one higher than it actually is when determining what effects they gain.

THE TRIPTYCH WHIP

Created in the nascent days of Commorragh's arenas, the Triptych Whip is a fusion of three masterfully balanced agonisers. Since then it has been borne by only a handful of Succubi, passed down to one skilled enough to slay its bearer in gladiatorial combat.

Succubus model equipped with an agoniser only. This Relic replaces an agoniser and has the following profile:

WEAPON	RANGE	TYPE	S	AP	D
The Triptych Whip	Melee	Melee	User	-3	2

Abilities: Poisoned Weapon (2+) (pg 89). Each time the bearer is selected to fight, add 3 to their Attacks characteristic until the end of the phase.

CRUSADE RULES

In this section you'll find additional rules for playing Crusade battles with Drukhari, such as Agendas, Battle Traits and Crusade Relics that are bespoke to DRUKHARI units. You can find out more about Crusade armies in the Warhammer 40,000 Core Book.

This section contains the following additional rules:

AGENDAS

DRUKHARI units attempt to achieve unique Agendas in Crusade battles, which can be found on the page opposite. These Agendas represent the unique goals of Drukhari raids on the battlefield and help to reflect their particular methods of waging war. You can find out more about Agendas in Crusade mission packs, such as that presented in the Warhammer 40,000 Core Book.

REQUISITIONS

Drukhari armies have access to a number of additional Requisitions, suited to the individual character of these sadistic murderers and torturers. You can find these on page 78.

BATTLE TRAITS

DRUKHARI units can be given one of the Battle Traits presented on page 79 as they gain experience and are promoted in your Crusade force. These help to better reflect the unique upgrades and Battle Honours that DRUKHARI units can gain.

TERRITORIAL DOMINANCE

If your army includes an ASCENDANT LORD unit, you can gain Raid Spoils points during your battles. You can spend these points to dominate areas of Commorragh and gain unique advantages. A list of territories that can be gained and the abilities they bestow can be found on pages 81-82.

WEAPON ENHANCEMENTS

DRUKHARI units equipped with poisoned weapons can select one of the Weapon Enhancements presented on page 84 as they are upgraded in your Crusade force. These contain specialist poisons with unique and deadly effects.

BATTLE SCARS

If a DRUKHARI unit gains a Battle Scar, you can select one from those presented on page 84. These Battle Scars represent the unique challenges and afflictions of the Drukhari, and help to add further character to your Crusade force.

CRUSADE RELICS

In addition to the Crusade Relics presented in the Warhammer 40,000 Core Book, Drukhari characters can claim one of the Crusade Relics described on page 85; these Relics are unique to the Drukhari, and grant the bearer both power and prestige.

SHOWCASE CRUSADE ARMY

On pages 86-87 you will find Chris Peach's superb Drukhari Crusade army, with a description of the force and its upgrades, and details of its exploits on the battlefield.

The webway gate opened with a flash of shimmering fuchsia and cerulean energy. Violet lightning crackled around its periphery as a handful of sleek, bladed craft shot through. Their flanks were deepest black, with harsh symbols painted a dark crimson. Complicated patterns and lattices on the crafts' surfaces resembled networks of capillaries. Sails rose up from the hulls and vicious-looking rams jutted out from their prows.

Thraed Xosh stood at the front of the foremost Raider. His thin lips curled into a smile, twisted out of shape by hideous scars that covered his face. Where his right eye should have been was an empty hole, bordered by shrivelled flesh.

No foe had come to meet them, nor had any rival.

My reascendancy begins here, he thought. He could hear warriors behind him preparing weapons, gloating about the kills they would make and the pain they would inflict. They had better be as good as they claimed to be. It had taken decades to acquire the wealth for even this meagre collection of battle craft, for which he had sunk to terrible depths of deprivation. All the pain, all the humiliation, all the suffering… all will be worth it, he told himself.

Xosh turned around to face his warriors. They were his Kabal – the Kabal of the Dying Night. The shadow that had covered him and sapped his fortunes would die today. Then, he thought, I will be death for those who cast me down to such depths.

'Our moment awaits where our rise begins, where our night of ignominy dies!', Xosh declared, projecting his voice to reach all the warriors aboard the skimmers. 'Each of you knows why you are here. Each of you has an insult to repay. Each of you hungers. This day, all will be satisfied.' There was no cheer, just three-dozen faces looking straight at him, every one promising painful retribution if he faltered in the smallest way.

The things I will do to any of you if you fail me, he swore to himself as he met each gaze. You will wish for She Who Thirsts before I am finished.

'The settlement', shouted his Raiders' helmsman. Xosh turned again.

There it was, undefended and weak. Just as he had wanted. Just as he had promised. It had cost another small fortune for knowledge of this place, which had not been harvested for generations of its inhabitants' short-lived kind. The people had grown plump and complacent. Their horror would be magnified a hundredfold when they saw the Raiders. Xosh salivated at the thought of tasting their terror and screams.

He saw figures running. The populace had seen them. Xosh cared not, for now fear would grip them. Its sweet aroma was already on the air that whipped around his thin hair and Drukhari-skin cloak.

AGENDAS

If your Crusade army includes any **Drukhari** units, you can select one Agenda from the Drukhari Agendas, listed below. This is a new category of Agendas, and follows all the normal rules for Agendas (for example, when you select Agendas, you cannot choose more than one from each category).

A GRUESOME BOUNTY

Drukhari Agenda

Competition to partake in a realspace raid is vicious. Those who secure such a position know it to be a route to wealth and power. The flesh of those taken captive is owned by the raid's orchestrator – or by their shadowy patrons, backers and creditors – but participating warriors seen to be instrumental in such captures can bank on greater prestige, as well as more tangible assets doled out in the wake of a successful raid.

Keep a Captive tally for each **Drukhari** unit (excluding **Beast** units) from your army. At the end of each turn, add 1 to that unit's Captive tally if any enemy units were destroyed by a melee attack made by that unit that turn.

At the end of the battle, each unit gains 1 experience point for every mark on its Captive tally.

DEMONSTRATE SUPERIORITY

Drukhari Agenda

Drukhari commanders barely tolerate their rivals. They seek any opportunity to put their particular skills to use in reminding such upstarts just who is in charge of their temporary alliance.

If your army includes a Realspace Raid Detachment, keep a Superiority tally for all **<Kabal>** units in that Detachment, another for all the **<Wych Cult>** units in that Detachment, and another for all the **<Haemonculus Coven>** units in that Detachment. Each time an enemy unit is destroyed by an attack made by a **Realspace Raider** unit from your army, add 1 to the Superiority tally for that unit's sub-faction (e.g. Kabal, Wych Cult or Haemonculus Coven). At the end of the battle, the **Character** model from the sub-faction with the highest Superiority tally gains 3 experience points (unless that model is a named character), and you can nominate one other unit from that sub-faction to gain 3 experience points.

Example: At the end of the battle, the <Wych Cult> *units from your Realspace Raid Detachment have destroyed the most enemy units, and so have the highest tally. The* **Succubus** *model from that Detachment and one other* <Wych Cult> *unit gains 3 experience points.*

> 'We will rise from these depths; that I promise. You see those spires, where our rivals glut themselves on plunder amidst the greatest riches of the galaxy? One day we will rule them. They have not yet heard of us, but they will. They will know us one day, when we slide our blades across their necks.'
>
> - *Thraed Xosh, Kabal of the Dying Night*

TAKE CREDIT

Drukhari Agenda

Drukhari commanders learn early how best to inflate their own standing by taking the achievements of others and twisting them to their own advantage. Leading a large raid is the perfect opportunity to take credit for all manner of successes, real or not, and reap the political bounty they generate.

At the end of the battle, select one **Drukhari Character** model from your army, and make a note of the total number of experience points **Drukhari** units from your army gained from other Agendas.

- For every 2 experience points gained by other units, that **Character** unit gains 1 experience point (to a maximum of 4).
- If that **Character** is an **Ascendant Lord** (pg 80), then for every 5 experience points gained by other units, you gain 1 Raid Spoils point (pg 80).

SEND A MESSAGE

Drukhari Agenda

A common method of heightening terror amongst prey is to ensure the initial victims of the raid are exhibited in all manner of loathsome ways, sending a clear message that such a fate will be shared by the remaining defenders. Raising flayed captives on spikes, linking screaming victims into the enemy's vox-net or hanging dripping trophies that still moan through stitched lips from visible vantage points ensures the enemy knows exactly what fate awaits them.

Keep a Terror tally for each **Drukhari** unit in your army.

Drukhari Infantry and **Biker** units from your army can attempt the following action:

Redecorate (Action): At the end of your Movement phase, one unit from your army that is within 3" of an objective marker can start to perform this action. This action is completed at the end of your turn. If completed, add 1 to that unit's Terror tally. That objective is now 'Terrifying' and has the following ability:

Terrifying (Aura): While a unit (excluding **Drukhari** units) is within 6" of this objective, subtract 1 from the Leadership characteristic of models in that unit.

While an enemy unit is within 6" of a Terrifying objective, each time that enemy unit fails a Morale test, add 1 to the Terror tally of each **Drukhari** unit from your army that is within 6" of the same objective.

At the end of the battle, each unit gains 1 experience point for every mark on its Terror tally.

REQUISITIONS

If your Crusade force includes any **Drukhari** units, you can spend Requisition points (RPs) on any of the following Requisitions in addition to those presented in the Warhammer 40,000 Core Book.

LORD OF THE DARK CITY   1RP

The masters of each faction within the Dark City vie for power and influence above all else, and proudly flaunt their domination over rivals nobles, their competitors in the arena or their twisted contemporaries amongst the Covens.

Purchase this Requisition when an **Archon**, **Succubus** or **Haemonculus** unit from your Crusade force gains the Battle-hardened, Heroic or Legendary rank. That model is upgraded to a Lord of Commorragh as described on pages 50-51; increase its Power Rating accordingly and make a note on its Crusade card. You cannot purchase this Requisition if doing so would cause your total Power Level to exceed your Crusade force's Supply Limit.

CHOSEN OF THE MASTER   1RP

The superior rulers of Commorragh gift their most talented murderers and blade artists with the choicest wargear and influence, granting them a measure of their master's power – under the implicit guarantee of death should failure follow.

Purchase this Requisition when you add a **Kabalite Warriors** unit to your Order of Battle if your Crusade force already includes a **Master Archon** unit, when you add a **Wyches** unit to your Order of Battle if your Crusade force already includes a **Master Succubus** unit or when you add a **Wracks** unit to your Order of Battle if your Crusade force already includes a **Master Haemonculus** unit. That added unit is upgraded to a Favoured Retinue as described on page 52; increase its Power Rating accordingly and make a note on its Crusade card. You cannot purchase this Requisition if doing so would cause your total Power Level to exceed your Crusade force's Supply Limit, and you can only have one such unit in your Crusade army for each associated **Character** unit in your Crusade force.

You can only use this Requisition once for each **Master Archon**, **Master Succubus** or **Master Haemonculus** unit on your Order of Battle.

SOUL TRAP   1RP

Soul traps vary in size and appearance, from pyramidal prisms to jewelled skulls engraved with vampiric runes, but all serve to capture the spirit essence of powerful enemies and empower the bearer with stolen energies.

Purchase this Requisition once after a battle in which an enemy **Character** unit was destroyed by a melee attack made by an **Archon** model from your army. Add 1 Soul point to that **Archon** model's Crusade card. Once that model has 5 Soul points, you can remove them and add 1 to that model's Attacks, Strength, Toughness and Leadership characteristics. If you do so, increase that **Archon** model's Crusade points value by 2, and you cannot select that **Archon** model for this Requisition again.

PATRON OF THE KILLING ARTS   1RP

This twisted benefactor has invested significantly in the breathtaking skills of their favoured gladiators. As well as basking in the reflected glory of these Wyches, both within and without their arena, such contacts afford the patron the opportunity to avail themselves of the latest combat stimms, no matter the risk.

Purchase this Requisition during the Muster Armies step, if your army includes any <**Wych Cult**> units. Select one **Archon** or **Haemonculus** unit from your army. Until the end of the battle, that unit gains the Combat Drugs ability; increase its Power Rating by 1 until the end of the battle. You cannot use this Requisition if this would take you over the maximum Power Level allowed for the battle size being played.

A CONSTANT SOURCE OF DISAPPOINTMENT   1RP

Sometimes an example needs to be made, and those who have failed their commander find themselves thrust into the arena to be slaughtered or disposed of in some other suitably gruesome manner.

Purchase this Requisition after a battle, while you have an **Ascendant Lord** (pg 80) on your Order of Battle. Select a unit from your Order of Battle that has 2 or more Battle Scars. Remove that unit from your Order of Battle. You gain a number of Raid Spoils points (pg 80) equal to that unit's Crusade points total.

CLANDESTINE DEALINGS   1+RP

The lords of the Kabals know all manner of methods to launder the various currencies of their trade throughout the Dark City. Whether this is rounding up captives from the slums to sell to the arenas or coercing dock workers to redirect cargo to their own holdings, no machination is below them.

Purchase this Requisition after a battle while you have an **Ascendant Lord Archon** (pg 80) on your Order of Battle after gaining Raid Spoils points (pg 80) for that battle. Gain a number of Raid Spoils points equal to the number of Requisition points spent on this Requisition.

BATTLE TRAITS

When a **Drukhari** unit gains a Battle Trait, you can use one of the tables below instead of one of the tables in the Warhammer 40,000 Core Book to determine what Battle Trait the unit has gained. To do so, roll one D6 and consult the appropriate table to randomly determine what Battle Trait the unit gains, or choose a Battle Trait that tells the best narrative for your unit. All the normal rules for Battle Traits apply (e.g. a unit cannot have the same Battle Trait more than once). As with any Battle Honour, make a note on the unit's Crusade card when it gains a Battle Trait and increase its Crusade points accordingly, as described in the Warhammer 40,000 Core Book.

CHARACTER UNITS

D6	TRAIT
1-2	**Perfectionist** *As much to raise themselves above their peers as to crush ambitious hopes of any beneath them, this lord of Commorragh refines their skills constantly, ensuring they are perceived as the pinnacle of their chosen obsession.* If an Agenda would ask you to keep a tally, at the start of the Update Crusade Cards step, add 1 to one tally you are keeping for this model.
3-4	**Proficient Predator** *This raid artisan has hunted the lesser races of the galaxy for millennia. They understand well the pain centres of their prey, and exert the precise amount of force necessary to subdue victims for their slave barges.* Once per turn, you can re-roll a single hit roll, wound roll, damage roll or saving throw made for this model.
5-6	**Lord of Toxins** *This creature has access to some of the most virulent toxins in all of Commorragh. The hyperfine molecular structure of these venoms allows them to pass through bonded ceramite after the merest of scratches.* Each time this model makes a melee attack, an unmodified wound roll of 6 inflicts 1 mortal wound on the target in addition to any normal damage.

<Wych Cult> INFANTRY AND <Wych Cult> BIKER UNITS

D6	TRAIT
1-2	**Fluid Encirclement** *Invigorated by the scent of a kill, these gladiators throw themselves into the fray with excessive energy.* Each time this unit makes a pile-in move, you can move each model up to 6".
3-4	**Master Flensers** *These performance killers are all experts with a blade, able to slay any victim in a flurry of darting knives.* Improve the Weapon Skill characteristic of models in this unit by 1.
5-6	**Lightning Strikes** *Once amongst the foe, these combatants flash their blades in the blink of an eye, opening veins and severing limbs.* Each time you make a melee attack for a model in this unit, an unmodified hit roll of 6 scores one additional hit.

KABALITE WARRIOR UNITS

D6	TRAIT
1-2	**Skilled Raiders** *These enforcers have mastered superb balance, instinctively rolling with every subtle pitch of their grav-transport, while punishing the foe with deadly accurate fire.* When this unit is selected to shoot with while embarked on a **Transport** unit, each time a model in this unit makes a ranged attack, you can ignore any or all modifiers to the hit roll.
3-4	**Ambitious Servants** *Seeking ever greater favour, these warriors are driven to perform above and beyond even their extraordinary abilities when in the presence of their superiors.* While this unit is within 6" of a friendly <Kabal> Archon unit, each time an attack is made by a model in this unit, re-roll a wound roll of 1.
5-6	**Privileged Position** *Through guile, effrontery and threats, these Kabalites ensure they are among the first to benefit from the revitalising anguish of any captives.* Out of Action tests taken for this unit are automatically passed.

<Haemonculus Coven> INFANTRY AND <Haemonculus Coven> MONSTER UNITS

D6	TRAIT
1-2	**Razorbone Spurs** *The sharpened bones of these creatures protrude through their calloused skin, and are laced with seeping, toxic marrow.* Each time an enemy unit finishes a charge move within Engagement Range of this unit, roll one D6: on a 2+, that enemy unit suffers 1 mortal wound.
3-4	**Multi-steroid Glands** *These fleshy nodules hang like ripe fruit from bony protrusions. At a Haemonculus' instigation, they pump a cocktail of metabolism enhancers into the bearers.* At the start of each battle, you can roll one D3 on the Combat Drugs table. This unit gains the ability listed under the result.
5-6	**Psychotraumic Brands** *The gnarled flesh of these creatures is imprinted with glowing sigils, burning into the minds of nearby psychic beings.* This unit has the following ability: '**Psychotraumic Brands (Aura):** While an enemy **Psyker** unit is within 6" of this unit, subtract 2 from Psychic tests made for that unit.'

TERRITORIAL DOMINANCE

Drukhari raids provide many valuable spoils. Worthy captives, trophies of exotic kills and stolen soul-fragments are among the most desirable resources hauled back to Commorragh. Power-hungry lords trade portions of these spoils to gain leverage, or to simply bribe interested parties, allowing them to bring more of the Dark City's nightmarish districts under their own control. But this is a dangerous game – as their power grows, so do the chances that a rival or even an agent of the Supreme Overlord will attempt to forcibly remind them of their place.

One **CHARACTER** model on your Order of Battle (excluding named characters) can be designated as an Ascendant Lord. That model gains the **ASCENDANT LORD** keyword. Your Crusade force can only include one **ASCENDANT LORD** unit. If you wish to change your Ascendant Lord, the previous one must first be removed from your Order of Battle. While you have an **ASCENDANT LORD** unit on your Order of Battle, after each battle, roll one D6: on a 4+, you gain one Raid Spoils point. If you won that battle, gain one additional Raid Spoils point. Raid Spoils can also be gained by other methods (Agendas etc.). Raid Spoils represent the various plunder taken while raiding realspace, and can be traded in for favours, influence, territory and many other things powerful Drukhari desire.

Keep a note of your Raid Spoil points total on your Order of Battle (the Crusade goals, notes and additional information box on your Order of Battle is a good place to keep track of this). If your Ascendant Lord is removed from your Order of Battle, all your current Raid Spoils points are lost.

If your Order of Battle contains an **ASCENDANT LORD** unit, you can spend Raid Spoils points to use the Dominate ability below to enable your Lord to claim dominance over a new territory in Commorragh, and to use the abilities listed under Spoils of Battle on page 83. Each ability will tell you how many Raid Spoils points must be spent to use it. When you use any of these abilities, delete any Raid Spoils points spent from your Order of Battle.

DOMINATE (1 RAID SPOILS POINT)

Your Lord uses a portion of their influence to strike at a target of opportunity, ousting its incumbent owners and taking it for their own.

You can randomly generate one territory from the tables opposite by first rolling a D6 to select one of the two tables (on a 1-3, use table 1; on a 4-6, use table 2), before rolling a D66 on that table (to roll a D66, roll two D6s, one after the other – the first result is your 'tens' and the second is your 'units'. For example, a D66 roll where the first result is a 3 and the second is a 6 is a result of 36).

Each territory is unique and cannot be selected or randomly generated more than once for your Ascendant Lord. If you randomly generate a territory that is already controlled by your Ascendant Lord, generate another. Keep a note of any territories claimed on your Order of Battle alongside your Raid Spoils total.

After gaining a new territory, roll one D6: on a 1, an assassination attempt is made on their life. Your **ASCENDANT LORD** unit gains one Battle Scar.

D66	TERRITORIES TABLE 1
11	The Splinterforge (Weapon Forge)
12	The Hall of Hooks (Weapon Forge)
13	The Sharpeners (Weapon Forge)
14	The Murder Cove (Weapon Forge)
15	Talonforge (Weapon Forge)
16	The Gallery of Blades (Weapon Forge)
21	Sorrowseep (Toxin Distillery)
22	Well of Phantasms (Toxin Distillery)
23	The Gland (Toxin Distillery)
24	Vale of Vapours (Toxin Distillery)
25	Tormentia's Boutique (Toxin Distillery)
26	The Fractal Alembic (Toxin Distillery)
31	Howling Gulf (Arena)
32	Mesmoria (Arena)
33	The Flensing Ground (Arena)
34	The Coreloop Gauntlet (Arena)
35	The Gallery of Glass (Arena)
36	Rethvhyr's Veinyard (Arena)
41	Spire of the Seven Talons (Scourge Spire)
42	The Screaming Roost (Scourge Spire)
43	The Gorenests (Scourge Spire)
44	The Pinion (Scourge Spire)
45	The Stratus Sphere (Scourge Spire)
46	Bladefeather Den (Scourge Spire)
51	The Bloodrazor (Incubi Shrine)
52	Shrine of the Naked Hatred (Incubi Shrine)
53	Shrine of the Cursed Night (Incubi Shrine)
54	The Covenant of Anguish (Incubi Shrine)
55	Shrine of the Crimson Hundred (Incubi Shrine)
56	Shrine of The Severed (Incubi Shrine)
61	Crimson Point (Docks)
62	Shardbreak (Docks)
63	Bleakharbour (Docks)
64	Blodhavn (Docks)
65	The Whisperdome (Docks)
66	Dock of Thieves (Docks)

D66	TERRITORIES TABLE 2
11	Drudge Pit (Sprawl Slum)
12	The Choke (Sprawl Slum)
13	Sufferer's Row (Sprawl Slum)
14	The Fiendscape (Sprawl Slum)
15	The Parchway (Sprawl Slum)
16	Vect's Heel (Sprawl Slum)
21	The Whispers (Trading District)
22	The Emporium of Tears (Trading District)
23	The Skinmongers (Trading District)
24	The Nervery (Trading District)
25	The Fleshpits (Trading District)
26	Traitor's Auction (Trading District)
31	The Evergloom (Shadow District)
32	Direside (Shadow District)
33	The Twilight Aisle (Shadow District)
34	Netherweir (Shadow District)
35	The Eyelid (Shadow District)
36	Hope's Horizon (Shadow District)
41	Bleak Spiral (Noble Spire)
42	Ghal-Harrow (Noble Spire)
43	The Crimson Spine (Noble Spire)
44	The Bonehalls (Noble Spire)
45	Knife of the Muses (Noble Spire)
46	Grovenspire (Noble Spire)
51	The Splinters (Gang Territory)
52	Broken Noose (Gang Territory)
53	The Harrows (Gang Territory)
54	Backstab Alleys (Gang Territory)
55	Ebonspite Corner (Gang Territory)
56	Bladewrought Lanes (Gang Territory)
61	Ironveil Tontine (Raidcraft Workshop)
62	The Shadowloom (Raidcraft Workshop)
63	Forge of the Connoisseur (Raidcraft Workshop)
64	The Fear Smeltery (Raidcraft Workshop)
65	Blackforge (Raidcraft Workshop)
66	Wingcast Spire (Raidcraft Workshop)

TERRITORIAL ABILITIES

While your Ascendant Lord is claiming dominance over three or more territories from the same category on page 81, they have access to the ability listed below for that category. Some of these abilities will affect your army during the battle, while others will take effect before or after the battle. At the end of the Muster Armies step of each battle, if your **ASCENDANT LORD** unit is included on your army roster, you can select any number of the territorial abilities your Ascendant Lord has access to. Add 1 to your **ASCENDANT LORD** unit's total Crusade points for that battle for each territorial ability they are using. These abilities are active for that battle, and remain active until the start of the Select Battle Size step of your next battle.

Weapon Forges
This lord's string of arcane armourers and energy-wreathed testing facilities give them access to exotic weapons technologies.

Once per battle, if your **ASCENDANT LORD** is on the battlefield, you can use one Wargear Stratagem for 0 Command points.

Toxin Distilleries
Commanding hundreds of alchemists and venom refiners, this lord's Kabalites carry vials of experimental poisons.

Once per battle, in your Command phase, if your **ASCENDANT LORD** is on the battlefield, you can select one <KABAL> unit from your army. Until the end of the turn, any poisoned weapons this unit is equipped with gain the Poisoned Weapon (2+) ability.

Arenas
This lord owns several gladiatorial murder-complexes, whose inventive warriors fight all the harder to retain the patronage granted them, and its associated prestige.

In the Update Experience Points step, Each **WYCHES** unit that was part of your Crusade army for this battle gains 1 additional experience point.

Scourge Spires
Even the flocks of mercenary Scourges fear and salute this lord.

In the Update Experience Points step, Each **SCOURGES** unit that was part of your Crusade army for this battle gains 1 additional experience point.

Incubi Shrines
Only the most powerful can call upon the favoured of the shrines.

In the Update Experience Points step, Each **INCUBI** unit that was part of your Crusade army for this battle gains 1 additional experience point.

Docks
Control of trade in and out of Commorragh's many ports is essential to maintaining an iron grip over the rest of the city.

After each battle, when rolling to determine if a Raid Spoils point is gained, add 2 to the roll.

Sprawl Slums
When a deed needs doing, having a ready supply of those Drukhari desperate to elevate themselves can be very useful.

Each time you spend a Raid Spoils point, roll one D6: on a 6, that Raid Spoils point is refunded.

Trading Districts
Many goods, both mundane and esoteric pass through these regions. A percentage of the profits flows to this lord's coffers, along with any items of particular interest to them.

Once after each battle, you can use the Relic Requisition for 0RP.

Shadow Districts
This brazen lord has some influence over the sinister denizens of Aelindrach, and is able to negotiate the service of their most potent scions.

In the Update Experience Points step, Each **MANDRAKES** unit that was part of your Crusade army for this battle gains 1 additional experience point.

Noble Spires
Being in possession of such enviable estates means this lord is never short of fawning admirers, and ever seeks opportunities to refresh their stable of pets to showcase at the next ball.

Once per battle, if an enemy **WARLORD** is destroyed by a melee attack made by your **ASCENDANT LORD**, you can use the Pray They Don't Take You Alive Stratagem for 0 Command points.

Gang Territories
Given the correct incentives, these peerless street killers can be persuaded to leave their dens and accompany a lord's raid.

In the Update Experience Points step, Each **REAVERS** or **HELLIONS** unit that was part of your Crusade army for this battle gains 1 additional experience point.

Raidcraft Workshop
Workshops crafting the finest anti-grav craft are essential to any realspace raid. Owning the best means ones warriors are borne to battle more swiftly than those of rivals.

At the end of the battle, you can ignore one failed Out of Action test taken for a **DRUKHARI VEHICLE** unit from your army – that test is treated as having been passed instead.

SPOILS OF BATTLE

Power and influence has many uses outside of the acquisition of new territories. A cunning negotiator can barter the spoils of a raid for any number of useful services, supplies or favours.

In addition to using the Dominate ability, you can also spend Raid Spoils points on the following:

SPECIALIST SUPPLIES (1+ RAID SPOILS)

Haemonculi have few qualms about the sources of the most interesting and rare bio-samples they barter for, and will trade great swathes of their spoils in order to experiment with them on their thrall creations.

If your Order of Battle contains an **ASCENDANT LORD HAEMONCULUS** unit, after each battle you can select one **<HAEMONCULUS COVEN>** unit (excluding **VEHICLE** units) from your Order of Battle and spend any number of Raid Spoils points. That unit gains a number of experience points equal to the number of Raid Spoils points spent.

PERFECT SPECIMENS (3 RAID SPOILS)

Whether trading openly for a clutch of another lord's prized warriors or employing street gangs to abduct a rival's property, Haemonculi are always eager to acquire the most magnificent physiques to experiment on.

If your Order of Battle contains an **ASCENDANT LORD HAEMONCULUS** unit, when you add a **<HAEMONCULUS COVEN> CORE** unit to your Order of Battle you can spend 3 Raid Spoils points. If you do so, that added unit gains 6 experience points (and therefore gains the Blooded rank). Select one Battle Honour for them as normal.

JUST A REPLICA (1 RAID SPOILS)

Haemonculi engrossed in greater works have been known to surgically alter an underling into a facsimile of themselves. Such occasions allow the master to avoid unnecessary risk when their visible presence is required more than their scientific expertise, and the subservient Haemonculus is swiftly disposed of should they become too ambitious.

If an Out of Action test is failed for an **ASCENDANT LORD HAEMONCULUS** unit, you can spend 1 Raid Spoils point. If you do so, that test is treated as having been passed, but that **HAEMONCULUS** unit does not gain any experience points from that battle.

ASSERT AUTHORITY (1 RAID SPOIL)

The best method of accumulating new territory for oneself is to take it from ones closest rivals, thus ensuring that as your power grows, theirs diminishes.

If your Order of Battle contains an **ASCENDANT LORD ARCHON** unit, if you win a battle against an army that includes an **ASCENDANT LORD** unit, you can select one territory that Ascendant Lord controls. Add that territory to your list of territories claimed. Your opponent must remove it from their list of territories claimed.

EXPERT MANIPULATION (3 RAID SPOILS)

Archons are well practiced at playing the long game, drawing out labyrinthine plans to outwit their foes. Once they set their gaze upon something, they will bribe, extort and threaten all who stand in their way of acquiring it.

If your Order of Battle contains an **ASCENDANT LORD ARCHON** unit, once after each battle you can spend 3 Raid Spoils points to select one territory from the Territories table (pg 81). Add that territory to your list of territories claimed.

COMPLEX RAIDCRAFTING (1 RAID SPOILS)

This master schemer has many aims and objectives, and by passing on bribes is able to ensure that their underlings each know exactly what is expected of them.

If your Order of Battle contains an **ASCENDANT LORD ARCHON** unit, before a battle, spend 1 Raid Spoils point. You can select 1 additional Agenda for your army for that battle.

INCREASE HOLDINGS (2 RAID SPOILS)

The best way to showcase your Cult's skills is to ensure you control as many of Commorragh's many arenas as possible. Giving your own fighters top billing and relegating your rivals to supporting slots at unfavourable events ensures your prestige grows unimpeded.

If your Order of Battle contains an **ASCENDANT LORD SUCCUBUS** unit, once after each battle you can spend 2 Raid Spoils points to select one Arena territory from the Territories table (pg 81). Add that territory to your list of territories claimed.

THE DEADLIEST CATCH (3 RAID SPOILS)

Using her contacts, this Succubus ensures she knows when new and exotic beasts are likely to arrive at Commorragh's many docks, and can work to ensure the very best of these find their way into her holding pens.

If your Order of Battle contains an **ASCENDANT LORD SUCCUBUS** unit, when you add a **DRUKHARI BEAST** unit to your Order of Battle, you can spend 3 Raid Spoils points. If you do so, that unit gains the Razor-edged, Brutal, Shredder or Fleshbane Weapon Enhancement Battle Honour (see Warhammer 40,000 Core Book). Increase that unit's Crusade points total by 1.

PERSONAL SUPPLY (1 RAID SPOILS)

Through both threats and demonstrations of explosive violence directed at their personal network of contacts, this Succubus ensures a greater supply of the most powerful stimulants.

If your Order of Battle contains an **ASCENDANT LORD SUCCUBUS** unit, when you randomly determine Combat Drugs abilities for a unit you can spend 1 Raid Spoils point. If you do so, you can re-roll one or both of the results.

WEAPON ENHANCEMENTS

When a **Drukhari** unit gains a Weapon Enhancement, you can, if the weapon selected is a poisoned weapon (pg 89), use the table below instead of one of the tables in the Warhammer 40,000 Core Book. Once you have selected the weapon, roll one D6 and consult the table to randomly determine what Weapon Enhancement is gained, or choose the one that tells the best narrative for your unit. All the normal rules for Weapon Enhancements still apply. As with any Battle Honour, make a note on the unit's Crusade card when it gains a Weapon Enhancement and increase its Crusade points accordingly, as described in the Warhammer 40,000 Core Book.

POISONED WEAPON ENHANCEMENTS

D6	ENHANCEMENT
1	**Feralex** *Those infected with this venom find themselves lashing out uncontrollably at all around them. Allies look on in terror as they are struck down by frenzied death throes.* Once per turn, at the end of your Shooting phase or the Fight phase, select one enemy unit that had any models destroyed by an attack made with this weapon this phase and roll one D6: on a 4+, that enemy unit suffers D3 mortal wounds.
2	**Shattergift** *This venom causes any psychic activity to send shards of agony through the victim's mind, disrupting aetheric abilities.* Once per turn, at the end of your Shooting phase or the Fight phase, select one enemy unit that had any models destroyed by an attack made with this weapon this phase. Until the start of your next turn, each time that unit attempts to manifest a psychic power, subtract 3 from the Psychic test.
3	**Agonite** *This venom spreads waves of agony so intense that even the most robust physiologies are overwhelmed with pain.* Each time an attack is made with this weapon, rules that ignore wounds cannot be used.
4	**Nerveshard** *This toxin overloads the victim's synapses, their drawn out agonised screams sending their allies fleeing in terror.* Each model that is destroyed by an attack made with this weapon counts as two models in the Morale phase.
5	**Icevein** *Once in the victim's bloodstream, this poison causes their dying flesh to radiate an intense chill that numbs their allies, preventing any swift escape from attackers.* Once per turn, at the end of your Shooting phase or the Fight phase, select one enemy unit that had any models destroyed by an attack made with this weapon this phase. Until the start of your next turn, halve the Move characteristic of models in that enemy unit and subtract 2 from Advance rolls and charge rolls made for that unit.
6	**Deathbloom** *A savagely applied dose of this toxin overloads the victim's organs with concentrated adrenal infusions that cause them to function so quickly that they rupture and burst in seconds.* Each time an attack is made with this weapon, an unmodified wound roll of 6 inflicts 1 mortal wound on the target in addition to any normal damage.

BATTLE SCARS

When a **Drukhari** unit gains a Battle Scar, you can select the relevant Battle Scar below instead of determining one from the Warhammer 40,000 Core Book. All the normal rules for Battle Scars apply (e.g. a unit cannot have the same Battle Scar more than once). As with any Battle Scar, make a note on the unit's Crusade card, but unlike other Battle Scars, do not decrease a unit's Crusade points for acquiring one of the Battle Scars listed below.

BATTLE SCARS

UNIT	BATTLE SCAR
Character unit only	**Insensate** *This warrior has become so jaded that their capacity to experience pain, pleasure or the anguish of others is diminished, slowly driving them mad with deprivation.* • Each time an attack is allocated to this model, halve the Damage characteristic of that attack. • This unit cannot use the Power From Pain ability.
Kabalite Warriors unit only	**Excommunicate** *Having committed some grave sin against their Kabal, these warriors attempt to strike out on their own, selling their services to the highest bidder.* This unit loses the <**Kabal**> keyword and gains the **Blades for Hire** keyword.
<**Wych Cult**> **Infantry** or <**Wych Cult**> **Biker** unit only	**Biochemical Hypershock** *Having overused countless combat stimulants, the bodies of these artistes are ravaged by chemicals. No longer in control of their effects, they suffer catastrophic physiological breakdowns.* • When determining the abilities granted by this unit's Combat Drugs ability, you cannot select an ability, you must randomly determine 2. • Subtract 1 from the Toughness and Leadership characteristics of models in this unit.
<**Haemonculus Coven**> **Infantry** unit only	**Cautionary Results** *Haemonculi are frequently experimental in their surgery, especially if their patients have displeased them. Not all of the outcomes of these surgeries are favourable, but they certainly ensure greater loyalty.* • Each time a model in this unit makes an attack, subtract 1 from that attack's hit roll. • Add 1 to the Strength and Leadership characteristics of models in this unit.

Amidst a Genestealer Cult uprising, Wyches from the Cult of the Red Grief intercept a force of roving saboteurs. Dropping from the overcast skies with shocking speed, their aerial hunters seek hybrid specimens with which to restock their arena's cells.

CRUSADE RELICS

When a **Drukhari Character** model gains a Crusade Relic, you can instead select one of the Relics listed below. All the usual rules for selecting Crusade Relics, as described in the Warhammer 40,000 Core Book, apply.

ARTIFICER RELIC

A **Drukhari Character** model can be given the following Artificer Relic instead of one of the ones presented in the Warhammer 40,000 Core Book.

Soulshard Grenade

Crafted from the captured spirit stones of Aeldari psykers, this grenade houses a soul that has been tortured to the point of madness. When thrown into the foe, the housing shatters and the mindless soul within lashes out, enacting revenge on the first living thing it can find.

Once per battle, at the end of your Movement phase, the bearer can use this Relic. If it does so, select one enemy unit within 6" of the bearer and roll a number of D6 equal to the number of models in that unit (to a maximum of 15). **Character** units count as 5 models and **Vehicle** and **Monster** units count as 10. If that enemy unit is a **Psyker**, add 1 to each result. For each result of 6+, that enemy unit suffers 1 mortal wound.

ANTIQUITY RELIC

A **Drukhari Character** model of Heroic rank or higher can be given the following Antiquity Relic instead of one of the ones presented in the Warhammer 40,000 Core Book. Add 1 to a unit's total Crusade points for each Antiquity Relic it has – this is in addition to the +1 from gaining a Battle Honour, for a total of +2.

Master Clone Field

While some influential figures in Commorragh can claim to own a clone field, this peerless example is said to be the first ever created. It projects multiple hologram-like images, which mimic the wearers movements perfectly. Enemies find their attacks absorbed by the simulacra, distracting them long enough for their true target to close in and strike a killing blow.

- The bearer has a 4+ invulnerable save.
- If the bearer is the target of a melee attack, after that enemy unit has fought, if it is still within Engagement Range, the bearer can make 2 melee attacks. These attacks must target that enemy unit.

LEGENDARY RELIC

A **Drukhari Character** model of Legendary rank can be given the following Legendary Relic instead of one of the ones presented in the Warhammer 40,000 Core Book. In addition, in order to give a model a Legendary Relic, you must also pay 1 Requisition point (if you do not have enough Requisition points, you cannot give that model a Legendary Relic). Add an additional 2 to a unit's total Crusade points for each Legendary Relic it has – this is in addition to the +1 from gaining a Battle Honour, for a total of +3.

Mask of the First Age

This intricately decorated mask is thought to date from the founding of the oldest pleasure cults, and was worn at ostentatious sensation-banquets by nobles who wished to display their power openly. Ownership of such a relic, and the nerve-shredding empathic technologies contained within, is a potent symbol of the wearer's influence.

This model has the following abilities:
- Add 1 to the bearer's Movement, Attacks, Wounds and Leadership characteristics.
- **Aura of Dominance (Aura):** While a unit is within 6" of this model, each time a Morale test is made for that unit, you can choose whether that test is passed or failed.

CRUSADE ARMY

Known to many as a regular Warhammer TV presenter, Chris Peach is also a diabolical mastermind of the Dark City. His force of Drukhari is themed around Wyches from the Cult of the Red Grief, with each element reinforcing the story.

Chris' Drukhari are a representation of the Circle of the Bloodied Blade, one of the Red Grief's constituent coteries of gladiators. For him, the excitement lies less with their exploits raiding the wider galaxy, and more with what they get up to when they return to the Cult's grand arena and the grisly spectacles they enact for their baying audiences. Most of the force's elements are those Chris feels would not be out of place fighting over bloody sands before a huge crowd, and he has modelled his bases to match: with gritty debris and the odd pool of soaked-in gore. The unit of Wracks, for instance, Chris sees as being paid to stitch fallen gladiators back together as well as experiment on those victims who fall to the Wyches' blades.

Chris has already named the primary characters in his ongoing narrative. Among them is his Archon, Pe'Ach the Cruel, who represents him personally on the tabletop. Chris conceived the idea that the warrior once held power in the upper echelons of Commorragh. Thanks to a strong survival instinct, Pe'Ach has now allied himself with the Wyches of the Bloodied Blade. Some of the Archon's retainers yet remain loyal to him, and Chris accompanies his avatar in battle with the remnants of the noble's court. Amongst such a coterie of blademasters, lightning-fast Reavers and highly mobile transports, he needs eyes everywhere. Chris imagines Pe'Ach's relationship with the Cult to be the healthy, Commorrite norm, with lots of backstabbing, butchery and mutual distrust!

Chris' favourite aspect of collecting the force has been the conversions among his Wyches. He has mixed and matched elements from several Drukhari kits, and even those from other factions, to give a varied and unique look to them all, hinting at the excessive variety of opponents they have fought against. Chris has even added a Wych riding atop his Razorwing Jetfighter. He imagines she steers the aircraft through some neural link with the pilot, executing stunning manoeuvres to decapitate warriors with the craft's wingtips. He has ideas of adding a whole menagerie of beasts and creatures that his Wyches test their blades against in the arena, or that hunt alongside a Beastmaster. While some of Chris' Crusade games will represent raids outside the Dark City as his warriors collect victims for use in the arena, other games could represent huge shows in the arena itself, as his Wyches cruelly hunt down captives within a mocking recreation of their home planet.

DATASHEETS

This section contains the datasheets that you will need to fight battles with your Drukhari miniatures, as well as details of army-specific abilities. You can find out how to use datasheets in the Warhammer 40,000 Core Book.

THE <KABAL>, <WYCH CULT> AND <HAEMONCULUS COVEN> KEYWORDS

Many datasheets in this section have either the <KABAL>, <WYCH CULT> or <HAEMONCULUS COVEN> keyword. These are keywords that you can select for yourself, as described in the Warhammer 40,000 Core Book, with the guidance detailed below.

When you include a <KABAL>, <WYCH CULT> or <HAEMONCULUS COVEN> unit in your army, you must nominate which Kabal, Wych Cult or Haemonculus Coven it is from and then replace the <KABAL>, <WYCH CULT> or <HAEMONCULUS COVEN> keyword in every instance on its datasheet with the name of your chosen Kabal, Wych Cult or Haemonculus Coven.

Example: If you include a Succubus in your army, and you decide she is from the Red Grief Wych Cult, her <WYCH CULT> keyword becomes RED GRIEF *and her Brides of Death ability reads, 'While a friendly* RED GRIEF CORE *unit is within 6" of this model, each time a model in that unit makes a melee attack, re-roll a wound roll of 1.'*

If your army is Battle-forged, you can only include units from one <KABAL>, one <WYCH CULT> and one <HAEMONCULUS COVEN> in the same Detachment. You can find out more about Battle-forged armies in the Warhammer 40,000 Core Book.

The datasheets for some units, such as Raiders or Venoms, may contain two or more of these keywords. Where this is the case, you must select one of these <KABAL>, <WYCH CULT> or <HAEMONCULUS COVEN> keywords to use before replacing that keyword with the name of your chosen Kabal, Wych Cult or Haemonculus Coven, as described above. The keywords that are not chosen are ignored.

WEAPON PROFILES

The weapon profiles found on a unit's datasheet describe the primary weapons that models in that unit can be equipped with. Some weapons are only referenced on a datasheet; profiles for these, and all other weapons, can be found on pages 116-118.

ABILITIES

A unit's datasheet will list all the abilities it has. Certain abilities that are common to many units are only referenced on the datasheets rather than described in full. These abilities are described below.

Power From Pain

As the Drukhari feed on the souls of the slain, they become imbued with supernatural might, eventually turning into killing machines.

This ability only applies if every unit in your army is a **DRUKHARI** or **UNALIGNED** unit. At the start of each battle round, this ability gains additional effects. These effects are cumulative.

POWER FROM PAIN

BATTLE ROUND	ADDITIONAL EFFECT
1+	**Inured to Suffering:** Models in this unit have a 6+ invulnerable save.
2+	**Eager to Flay:** This unit is eligible to declare a charge in a turn in which they Advanced.
3+	**Flensing Fury:** Each time a model in this unit makes a melee attack, add 1 to that attack's hit roll. If this unit has the **VEHICLE** or **MONSTER** keyword, it does not suffer the penalty incurred to its hit rolls for firing Heavy weapons at enemy units that are within Engagement Range of it.
4+	**Mantle of Agony:** Models in this unit have a 5+ invulnerable save.
5+	**Emboldened by Bloodshed:** Each time a Morale test is taken for this unit, it is automatically passed. If this unit's characteristics can change as it suffers damage, this unit is considered to have double the number of wounds remaining for the purposes of determining what those characteristics are.

Poisoned Weapon

The Drukhari frequently use virulent poisons to kill their prey in excruciating ways.

Many Drukhari weapons have the Poisoned Weapon ability. Such a weapon will have an ability that reads 'Poisoned Weapon' and then a value, such as (4+) or (2+). Each time an attack is made with a poisoned weapon against a unit (excluding **VEHICLE** or **TITANIC** units), an unmodified wound roll of this value is always successful.

Blade Artists

Every denizen of Commorragh learns from a young age the value of blades, and all are adept in their usage, whether those wielded by their cruel hands or as part of their razor-edged armour.

Each time a model in this unit makes an attack with a melee weapon, on an unmodified wound roll of 6, improve the Armour Penetration characteristic of that attack by 1.

Insensible to Pain

The exquisite agonies visited upon the minions of the Haemonculus Covens have ensured that even the lowliest Wrack is oblivious to the most potent of weaponry.

Each time a model in this unit would lose a wound, roll one D6: on a 5+, that wound is not lost.

Combat Drugs

Exotic chemical stimulants are widely used to heighten combat performance, despite the risk of a deadly overdose.

Units with this ability gain additional abilities depending on which combat drugs they are using during this battle. Before the battle, determine what additional abilities are granted to each unit from your army with the Combat Drugs ability. You can select one of the abilities from the table below for that unit. Alternatively, you can randomly determine two abilities from the table for units with the Combat Drugs ability by rolling two D6 and looking up the result (if a double is rolled, roll both dice again until two different results are rolled). Combat Drug effects must be noted on your army roster. If you wish to randomly determine a unit's Combat Drugs abilities, simply write 'Random' on your roster.

COMBAT DRUGS

D6	COMBAT DRUGS
1	**Adrenalight:** Each time this unit fights, if it made a charge move or performed a Heroic Intervention this turn, then until that fight is resolved, add 1 to the Attacks characteristic of models in this unit.
2	**Grave Lotus:** Add 1 to the Strength characteristic of models in this unit.
3	**Hypex:** Add 2" to the Move characteristic of models in this unit.
4	**Painbringer:** Add 1 to the Toughness characteristic of models in this unit.
5	**Serpentin:** Improve the Weapon Skill characteristic of models in this unit by 1.
6	**Splintermind:** Improve the Ballistic Skill and Leadership characteristics of models in this unit by 1.

ARCHON

No.	Name	M	WS	BS	S	T	W	A	Ld	Sv
1	Archon	8"	2+	2+	3	3	5	5	9	4+

An Archon is equipped with: splinter pistol; power sword.

WEAPON	RANGE	TYPE	S	AP	D	ABILITIES
Blast pistol	6"	Pistol 1	8	-4	D6	-
Splinter pistol	12"	Pistol 1	2	0	1	Poisoned Weapon (4+) (pg 89)
Agoniser	Melee	Melee	User	-3	1	Poisoned Weapon (4+) (pg 89)
Huskblade	Melee	Melee	User	-2	2	-
Power sword	Melee	Melee	+1	-3	1	-
Venom blade	Melee	Melee	User	-1	1	Poisoned Weapon (2+) (pg 89)

WARGEAR OPTIONS

- This model's power sword can be replaced with one of the following: 1 agoniser; 1 huskblade; 1 venom blade.
- This model's splinter pistol can be replaced with 1 blast pistol.

ABILITIES

Blade Artists, Power From Pain (pg 89)

Overlord (Aura): While a friendly <Kabal> Core or Incubi unit is within 6" of this model, each time an attack is made by a model in that unit, re-roll a hit roll of 1.

Shadowfield: This model has a 2+ invulnerable save. This invulnerable saving throw can never be re-rolled. The first time this invulnerable saving throw is failed, until the end of the battle, this ability has no effect.

FACTION KEYWORDS: Aeldari, Drukhari, <Kabal>
KEYWORDS: Infantry, Character, Archon

Archons apply the same inventive malice with which they rule the fractured Kabals to their enemies on the battlefield. Leading many realspace raids, Archons arrogantly dare their enemies to face their martial expertise, their arsenal of eldritch weapons and the labyrinthine cunning that has enabled their rise to power.

SUCCUBUS

3 POWER

No.	Name	M	WS	BS	S	T	W	A	Ld	Sv
1	Succubus	8"	2+	2+	3	3	5	6	8	6+

A Succubus is equipped with: agoniser; archite glaive.

WEAPON	RANGE	TYPE	S	AP	D	ABILITIES
Blast pistol	6"	Pistol 1	8	-4	D6	-
Splinter pistol	12"	Pistol 1	2	0	1	Poisoned Weapon (4+) (pg 89)
Agoniser	Melee	Melee	User	-3	1	Poisoned Weapon (4+) (pg 89)
Archite glaive	Melee	Melee	+2	-3	1	-

WARGEAR OPTIONS

- This model's agoniser and archite glaive can be replaced with one of the following: 1 hydra gauntlets; 1 razorflails; 1 shardnet and impaler.
- This model's agoniser can be replaced with one of the following: 1 blast pistol; 1 splinter pistol.

ABILITIES

Blade Artists, Combat Drugs, Power From Pain (pg 89)

Brides of Death (Aura): While a friendly <Wych Cult> Core unit is within 6" of this model, each time a model in that unit makes a melee attack, re-roll a wound roll of 1.

Lightning Dodge: This model has a 4+ invulnerable save.

No Escape: Each time an enemy unit (excluding Titanic units) that is within Engagement Range of this model is selected to Fall Back, roll off with your opponent, subtracting 1 from your opponent's roll if this model is equipped with a shardnet and impaler. If you win, that unit cannot Fall Back this turn.

FACTION KEYWORDS: **Aeldari, Drukhari, <Wych Cult>**
KEYWORDS: **Infantry, Character, Succubus**

Succubi are the leaders of the Wych Cults and master combatants of the arena, possessing both sublime and bloody artistry. They are versed in countless forms of death and give visceral displays of acrobatic lethality. With lightning-fast reactions and a variety of outlandish weapons, they savour the greatest of foes and revel in their own superiority.

HAEMONCULUS

4 POWER

No.	Name	M	WS	BS	S	T	W	A	Ld	Sv
1	Haemonculus	7"	2+	2+	3	4	6	4	8	6+

A Haemonculus is equipped with: stinger pistol; haemonculus tools; ichor injector; scissorhand.

WEAPON	RANGE	TYPE	S	AP	D	ABILITIES
Stinger pistol	12"	Pistol 1	2	0	1	Poisoned Weapon (2+) (pg 89)
Haemonculus tools	Melee	Melee	User	0	1	Poisoned Weapon (2+) (pg 89)
Ichor injector	Melee	Melee	-	-	-	Each time the bearer fights, no more than one attack can be made with this weapon. Each time an attack is made with this weapon, if a hit is scored, the target suffers 1 mortal wound and the attack sequence ends.
Scissorhand	Melee	Melee	User	-2	1	Poisoned Weapon (4+) (pg 89). Each time the bearer fights, it makes 2 additional attacks with this weapon.

ABILITIES

Blade Artists, Insensible To Pain, Power From Pain (pg 89)

Master of Pain (Aura): While a friendly <Haemonculus Coven> Core unit is within 6" of any models with this ability, add 1 to the Toughness characteristic of models in that unit.

Fleshcraft: At the end of your Movement phase, select one <Haemonculus Coven> Monster or <Haemonculus Coven> Grotesques model from your army that is within 3" of this model. The model you selected regains D3 lost wounds. Each model can only be healed once per turn.

FACTION KEYWORDS: **Aeldari, Drukhari, <Haemonculus Coven>**
KEYWORDS: **Infantry, Character, Haemonculus**

Wielding arrays of horrific implements from their personal oubliettes and laboratories, Haemonculi drift like sinister predators in battle. They direct their Covens of twisted monstrosities and pain-adepts while hungrily seeking out fresh subjects for their hideous fleshcrafting.

LELITH HESPERAX

5 POWER

No.	Name	M	WS	BS	S	T	W	A	Ld	Sv
1	Lelith Hesperax	8"	2+	2+	3	3	5	7	8	6+

Lelith Hesperax is equipped with: Lelith's blades. Your army can only include one **LELITH HESPERAX** model.

WEAPON	RANGE	TYPE	S	AP	D	ABILITIES
Lelith's blades	Melee	Melee	+1	-3	1	Each time an attack is made with this weapon, an unmodified hit roll of 6 scores 1 additional hit.

ABILITIES

Blade Artists, Power From Pain (pg 89)

At Last, a Challenge: Each time this model makes a melee attack that targets a **CHARACTER** unit, you can re-roll the hit roll and you can re-roll the wound roll.

Brides of Death (Aura): While a friendly **CULT OF STRIFE CORE** unit is within 6" of this model, each time a model in that unit makes a melee attack, re-roll a wound roll of 1.

Quicksilver Dodge: This model has a 4+ invulnerable save. Each time a melee attack is made against this model, subtract 1 from that attack's hit roll.

Deadly Dance: Each time this model makes a consolidation move, it can move an additional 3", and it does not have to finish this move closer to the closest enemy model.

Natural Perfection: In your Command phase, select one of the following:

• **Thrilling Acrobatics:** Until the end of the turn, this model is eligible to declare a charge in a turn in which it Fell Back or Advanced.

• **Gory Spectacle:** In the Fight phase of this turn, if this model destroys any enemy models, then at the end of that phase it can fight again.

No Escape: Each time an enemy unit (excluding **TITANIC** units) that is within Engagement Range of this model is selected to Fall Back, roll off with your opponent. If you win, that unit cannot Fall Back this turn.

FACTION KEYWORDS: AELDARI, DRUKHARI, CULT OF STRIFE
KEYWORDS: INFANTRY, CHARACTER, SUCCUBUS, MASTER SUCCUBUS, LELITH HESPERAX

Lelith Hesperax's lithe athleticism is far beyond those of other Wyches. She has raised death to a high art, wielding nothing more than simple knives. Gifting her victims with precision wounds in an exotic blur of blade and flesh, she finishes in a bloody finale with a gory flourish.

Lelith Hesperax, Queen of Knives

DRAZHAR

7 POWER

No.	Name	M	WS	BS	S	T	W	A	Ld	Sv
1	Drazhar	7"	2+	2+	4	4	6	5	9	2+

Drazhar is equipped with: The Executioner's demiklaives. Your army can only include one **DRAZHAR** model.

WEAPON	RANGE	TYPE	S	AP	D	ABILITIES
The Executioner's demiklaives		Before selecting targets, select one of the profiles below to make attacks with.				
- Single blade	Melee	Melee	+2	-3	3	-
- Dual blades	Melee	Melee	+1	-3	2	Each time the bearer fights, if this weapon profile is selected, it makes 2 additional attacks with this weapon.

ABILITIES

Blade Artists, Power From Pain (pg 89)

Murderous Assault: This model can be selected to fight one additional time in each Fight phase. It must be eligible to fight each time it is selected to do so.

Ancient Warrior: Each time an attack is allocated to this model, subtract 1 from the Damage characteristic of that attack (to a minimum of 1).

Eternal Warrior: This model has a 4+ invulnerable save.

Tormentors: At the start of the Fight phase, select one enemy unit within Engagement Range of this model and roll 2D6: if the result is greater than the enemy unit's Leadership characteristic, until the end of the phase, that unit is not eligible to fight until after all eligible units from your army have done so.

Master of Blades (Aura): While a friendly **INCUBI** unit is within 6" of this model, each time a model in that unit makes a melee attack, add 1 to that attack's wound roll.

FACTION KEYWORDS: AELDARI, DRUKHARI, INCUBI
KEYWORDS: INFANTRY, CHARACTER, BLADES FOR HIRE, DRAZHAR

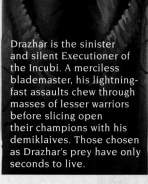

Drazhar is the sinister and silent Executioner of the Incubi. A merciless blademaster, his lightning-fast assaults chew through masses of lesser warriors before slicing open their champions with his demiklaives. Those chosen as Drazhar's prey have only seconds to live.

Drazhar, Master of Blades

93

URIEN RAKARTH

5 POWER

No.	Name	M	WS	BS	S	T	W	A	Ld	Sv
1	Urien Rakarth	7"	2+	2+	3	5	6	5	8	6+

Urien Rakarth is equipped with: Casket of Flensing; haemonculus tools; ichor injector. Your army can only include one **URIEN RAKARTH** model.

WEAPON	RANGE	TYPE	S	AP	D	ABILITIES
Casket of Flensing	12"	Assault 2D6	3	-2	1	The bearer can only shoot with this weapon once per battle. Each time an attack is made with this weapon, that attack automatically hits the target.
Haemonculus tools	Melee	Melee	User	0	1	Poisoned Weapon (2+) (pg 89)
Ichor injector	Melee	Melee	-	-	-	Each time the bearer fights, no more than one attack can be made with this weapon. Each time an attack is made with this weapon, if a hit is scored, the target suffers 1 mortal wound and the attack sequence ends.

ABILITIES

Blade Artists, Insensible to Pain, Power From Pain (pg 89)

Haemovores: At the start of the Fight phase, roll one D6 for each enemy unit within Engagement Range of this model: on a 6, that unit suffers 1 mortal wound.

Sustained by Dark Science: Once per battle, when this model is destroyed, you can choose to roll one D6 at the end of the phase instead of using any rules that are triggered when that model is destroyed. If you do so, then on a 2+, set this model back up on the battlefield as close as possible to where they were destroyed and not within Engagement Range of any enemy models, with D3 wounds remaining.

Fleshcraft: At the end of your Movement phase, select one **PROPHETS OF FLESH MONSTER** or **PROPHETS OF FLESH GROTESQUES** model from your army that is within 3" of this model. The model you selected regains D3 lost wounds. Each model can only be healed once per turn.

Clone Field: This model has a 4+ invulnerable save.

Contempt for Death: Each time an attack is allocated to this model, halve the Damage characteristic of that attack (rounding up).

Master of Pain (Aura): While a friendly **PROPHETS OF FLESH CORE** unit is within 6" of any models with this ability, add 1 to the Toughness characteristic of models in that unit.

Sculptor of Torments (Aura): While a friendly **PROPHETS OF FLESH CORE** unit is within 6" of this model, add 1 to the Strength and Leadership characteristics of models in that unit.

FACTION KEYWORDS: AELDARI, DRUKHARI, PROPHETS OF FLESH
KEYWORDS: INFANTRY, CHARACTER, HAEMONCULUS, MASTER HAEMONCULUS, URIEN RAKARTH

Urien Rakarth is the most ingenious of the many Haemonculi masters. He is the Sculptor of Torments, whose repugnant creations strain his enemies' sanity. Once his casket of fanged spirits and his toxin-laced blades are finished, a coiling nest of Haemovores feast upon whatever is left of Rakarth's foes.

KABALITE WARRIORS

3 POWER

No.	Name	M	WS	BS	S	T	W	A	Ld	Sv
4-19	Kabalite Warrior	7"	3+	3+	3	3	1	2	7	4+
1	Sybarite	7"	3+	3+	3	3	1	3	8	4+

If this unit contains between 6 and 10 models, it has **Power Rating 6**. If this unit contains between 11 and 15 models, it has **Power Rating 9**. If this unit contains between 16 and 20 models, it has **Power Rating 12**. Every model is equipped with: splinter rifle.

WEAPON	RANGE	TYPE	S	AP	D	ABILITIES
Blast pistol	6"	Pistol 1	8	-4	D6	-
Blaster	18"	Assault 1	8	-4	D6	-
Dark lance	36"	Heavy 1	8	-4	D3+3	-
Phantasm grenade launcher	18"	Assault D3	-	-	-	Blast. Each time a unit is hit by this weapon, roll 2D6. If the result is higher than the Leadership characteristic of that unit, it suffers 1 mortal wound.
Shredder	18"	Assault D6	6	-1	1	Blast
Splinter cannon	36"	Heavy 3	3	-1	2	Poisoned Weapon (4+) (pg 89)
Splinter pistol	12"	Pistol 1	2	0	1	Poisoned Weapon (4+) (pg 89)
Splinter rifle	24"	Rapid Fire 1	2	0	1	Poisoned Weapon (4+) (pg 89)
Agoniser	Melee	Melee	User	-3	1	Poisoned Weapon (4+) (pg 89)
Power sword	Melee	Melee	+1	-3	1	-

WARGEAR OPTIONS

- The Sybarite can be equipped with one of the following: 1 power sword; 1 agoniser.
- The Sybarite can be equipped with 1 phantasm grenade launcher.
- The Sybarite's splinter rifle can be replaced with one of the following: 1 splinter pistol; 1 blast pistol.
- For every 10 models in this unit, 1 Kabalite Warrior's splinter rifle can be replaced with one of the following: 1 dark lance; 1 splinter cannon.
- For every 5 models in this unit, 1 Kabalite Warrior's splinter rifle can be replaced with one of the following: 1 blaster; 1 shredder.

ABILITIES

Blade Artists, Power From Pain (pg 89)

FACTION KEYWORDS: AELDARI, DRUKHARI, <KABAL>
KEYWORDS: INFANTRY, CORE, KABALITE WARRIORS

Clad from head to foot in blade-edged, segmented armour, Kabalite Warriors are an intimidating, arachnoid presence. They are highly-skilled, cruel enforcers who unleash hails of toxin-coated shards during swift and agile advances, driving terrified prey before them at their master's whim.

Kabalite Warrior with shredder

Kabalite Warrior with splinter cannon

Kabalite Warrior with splinter rifle

Kabalite Warrior with dark lance

WYCHES

3 POWER

No.	Name	M	WS	BS	S	T	W	A	Ld	Sv
4-19	Wych	8"	3+	3+	3	3	1	3	7	6+
1	Hekatrix	8"	3+	3+	3	3	1	4	8	6+

If this unit contains between 6 and 10 models, it has **Power Rating 6**. If this unit contains between 11 and 15 models, it has **Power Rating 9**. If this unit contains between 16 and 20 models, it has **Power Rating 12**. Every model is equipped with: splinter pistol; Hekatarii blade; plasma grenades.

WEAPON	RANGE	TYPE	S	AP	D	ABILITIES
Blast pistol	6"	Pistol 1	8	-4	D6	-
Phantasm grenade launcher	18"	Assault D3	-	-	-	Blast. Each time a unit is hit by this weapon, roll 2D6. If the result is higher than the Leadership characteristic of that unit, it suffers 1 mortal wound.
Splinter pistol	12"	Pistol 1	2	0	1	Poisoned Weapon (4+) (pg 89)
Agoniser	Melee	Melee	User	-3	1	Poisoned Weapon (4+) (pg 89)
Hekatarii blade	Melee	Melee	User	-1	1	Each time the bearer fights, it makes 1 additional attack with this weapon.
Hydra gauntlets	Melee	Melee	+2	-2	1	Each time the bearer fights, it makes 1 additional attack with this weapon.
Power sword	Melee	Melee	+1	-3	1	-
Razorflails	Melee	Melee	User	-1	1	Each time an attack is made with this weapon, make 2 hit rolls instead of 1.
Shardnet and impaler	Melee	Melee	User	-2	2	Each time the bearer fights, it makes 1 additional attack with this weapon.
Plasma grenades	6"	Grenade D6	4	-1	1	Blast

WARGEAR OPTIONS

- The Hekatrix can be equipped with 1 phantasm grenade launcher.
- The Hekatrix's splinter pistol can be replaced with 1 blast pistol.
- The Hekatrix's Hekatarii blade can be replaced with one of the following: 1 power sword; 1 agoniser.
- If this unit contains 10 or more models:
  - 1 Wych's splinter pistol and Hekatarii blade can be replaced with 1 hydra gauntlets.
  - 1 Wych's splinter pistol and Hekatarii blade can be replaced with 1 razorflails.
  - 1 Wych's splinter pistol and Hekatarii blade can be replaced with 1 shardnet and impaler.
- If this unit contains 20 models:
  - 1 Wych's splinter pistol and Hekatarii blade can be replaced with 1 hydra gauntlets.
  - 1 Wych's splinter pistol and Hekatarii blade can be replaced with 1 razorflails.
  - 1 Wych's splinter pistol and Hekatarii blade can be replaced with 1 shardnet and impaler.

ABILITIES

Blade Artists, Combat Drugs, Power From Pain (pg 89)

Dodge: Models in this unit have a 6+ invulnerable save. Models in this unit have a 4+ invulnerable save against melee attacks.

No Escape: Each time an enemy unit (excluding TITANIC units) that is within Engagement Range of this unit is selected to Fall Back, roll off with your opponent, subtracting 1 from your opponent's roll for each model this unit contains equipped with a shardnet and impaler. If you win, that unit cannot Fall Back this turn.

FACTION KEYWORDS: AELDARI, DRUKHARI, <WYCH CULT>
KEYWORDS: INFANTRY, CORE, HAYWIRE GRENADE, WYCHES

The dancers of death, Wyches are acrobatic murder-artists, exhibiting their incredible arena skills to slay with precision and elan. They wield exotic weapons – hooks, barbed chains or flensing blades – that require superior ability. These are deadly in Wyches' hands as they dart, twist and blur around their foes' clumsy attacks.

WRACKS

3 POWER

No.	Name	M	WS	BS	S	T	W	A	Ld	Sv
4-19	Wrack	7"	3+	3+	3	4	1	2	7	6+
1	Acothyst	7"	3+	3+	3	4	1	3	8	6+

If this unit contains between 6 and 10 models, it has **Power Rating 6**. If this unit contains between 11 and 15 models, it has **Power Rating 9**. If this unit contains between 16 and 20 models, it has **Power Rating 12**. Every model is equipped with: Wrack blades.

WEAPON	RANGE	TYPE	S	AP	D	ABILITIES
Hexrifle	36"	Heavy 1	6	-2	2	Each time you select a target for this weapon, you can ignore the Look Out, Sir rule. Each time an attack is made with this weapon, an unmodified wound roll of 6 inflicts 1 mortal wound on the target in addition to any normal damage.
Liquifier gun	12"	Assault D6	4	-2	1	Each time an attack is made with this weapon, that attack automatically hits the target.
Ossefactor	24"	Assault 1	2	-3	2	Poisoned Weapon (2+) (pg 89)
Stinger pistol	12"	Pistol 1	2	0	1	Poisoned Weapon (2+) (pg 89)
Agoniser	Melee	Melee	User	-3	1	Poisoned Weapon (4+) (pg 89)
Electrocorrosive whip	Melee	Melee	2	-2	1	Poisoned Weapon (4+) (pg 89). Each time an attack is made with this weapon, make 2 hit rolls instead of 1.
Flesh gauntlet	Melee	Melee	+1	0	1	Each time an attack is made with this weapon, if the target is not a **Vehicle** unit, an unmodified wound roll of 6 inflicts 1 mortal wound on the target in addition to any normal damage.
Mindphase gauntlet	Melee	Melee	User	-1	2	-
Scissorhand	Melee	Melee	User	-2	1	Poisoned Weapon (4+) (pg 89). Each time the bearer fights, it makes 2 additional attacks with this weapon.
Venom blade	Melee	Melee	User	-1	1	Poisoned Weapon (2+) (pg 89)
Wrack blades	Melee	Melee	User	-1	1	Poisoned Weapon (4+) (pg 89)

WARGEAR OPTIONS

- For every five models this unit contains, one Wrack can be equipped with one of the following: 1 liquifier gun; 1 ossefactor.
- The Acothyst's Wrack blades can be replaced with one of the following: 1 agoniser; 1 electrocorrosive whip; 1 flesh gauntlet; 1 mindphase gauntlet; 1 scissorhand; 1 venom blade.
- The Acothyst can be equipped with one of the following: 1 hexrifle; 1 liquifier gun; 1 stinger pistol.

ABILITIES

Blade Artists, Insensible To Pain, Power From Pain (pg 89)

FACTION KEYWORDS: Aeldari, Drukhari, <Haemonculus Coven>
KEYWORDS: Infantry, Core, Wracks

The gnarled hide of the Wracks is a leathery mass of old scars, inured to pain. These adepts of fleshcrafting serve wizened masters of the Covens, and are as much experiments as they are apprentices. They are granted a host of gruesome tools, butchering blades and arcane bio-weapons with which they inflict maximum agony.

COURT OF THE ARCHON

5 POWER

No.	Name	M	WS	BS	S	T	W	A	Ld	Sv
0-4	Lhamaean	8"	3+	3+	3	3	3	2	8	5+
0-4	Medusae	8"	3+	3+	3	3	3	1	8	5+
0-4	Sslyth	8"	3+	3+	5	3	3	3	6	5+
0-4	Ur-Ghul	8"	3+	-	4	3	3	4	4	7+

This unit must contain at least 4 models. If this unit contains between 5 and 8 models, it has **Power Rating 10**. If this unit contains between 9 and 12 models, it has **Power Rating 15**. If this unit contains between 13 and 16, models it has **Power Rating 20**.

- Every Lhamaean is equipped with: shaimeshi blade.
- Every Medusae is equipped with: eyeburst.
- Every Sslyth is equipped with: shardcarbine; splinter pistol; Sslyth battle-blade.
- Every Ur-Ghul is equipped with: Ur-Ghul talons.

WEAPON	RANGE	TYPE	S	AP	D	ABILITIES
Eyeburst	12"	Pistol D6	4	-2	1	Each time an attack is made with this weapon, that attack automatically hits the target.
Shardcarbine	18"	Assault 3	2	0	1	Poisoned Weapon (4+) (pg 89)
Splinter pistol	12"	Pistol 1	2	0	1	Poisoned Weapon (4+) (pg 89)
Shaimeshi blade	Melee	Melee	User	0	1	Poisoned Weapon (2+) (pg 89). Each time an attack is made with this weapon, if the target is not a **VEHICLE** unit, an unmodified wound roll of 6 inflicts 1 mortal wound on the target in addition to any normal damage.
Sslyth battle-blade	Melee	Melee	User	-2	1	-
Ur-Ghul talons	Melee	Melee	User	-1	1	-

ABILITIES

Blade Artists (LHAMAEAN models only), **Power From Pain** (pg 89)

Court of the Archon: This unit can only be included in a Detachment if that Detachment also includes one or more **ARCHON** units, and you can only include a maximum of 1 **COURT OF THE ARCHON** units for each **ARCHON** unit in that Detachment. This unit does not take up slots in a Detachment.

Cold-blooded Bodyguard: While this unit contains any Sslyth models, while a friendly **ARCHON** unit is within 3" of this unit, enemy models cannot target that **ARCHON** unit with ranged attacks.

Resilient Species: Each time a Sslyth or Ur-Ghul model in this unit would lose a wound, roll one D6: on a 5+, that wound is not lost.

Ferocious Charge: Each time this unit fights, if it made a charge move this turn, add 2 to the Attacks characteristic of Ur-Ghul models in this unit.

Toxin Crafter (Aura): While a friendly <KABAL> ARCHON or <KABAL> KABALITE TRUEBORN unit is within 3" of this unit, if this unit contains any LHAMAEAN models, each time a model in that <KABAL> ARCHON or <KABAL> KABALITE TRUEBORN unit makes an attack with a poisoned weapon (pg 89) an unmodified hit roll of 6 automatically wounds the target.

FACTION KEYWORDS: **AELDARI, DRUKHARI, <KABAL>**
KEYWORDS: **INFANTRY, CORE, COURT OF THE ARCHON**

Nothing but the manipulative cunning of an Archon could demand the loyalty of their varied Courts. Drawn from diverse mercenary factions that inhabit Commorragh, Drukhari, aliens and other horrors protect their liege with all manner of twisted weapons, flesh-eating venoms, needle-like fangs and empathic leaching.

INCUBI

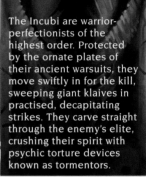

No.	Name	M	WS	BS	S	T	W	A	Ld	Sv
4-9	Incubus	7"	2+	3+	3	3	1	3	8	3+
1	Klaivex	7"	2+	3+	3	3	2	4	9	3+

If this unit contains 6 or more models, it has **Power Rating 8**. Every model is equipped with: klaive.

WEAPON	RANGE	TYPE	S	AP	D	ABILITIES
Demiklaives	Before selecting targets, select one of the profiles below to make attacks with.					
- Single blade	Melee	Melee	+2	-3	2	-
- Dual blades	Melee	Melee	+1	-2	2	Each time the bearer fights, if this weapon profile is selected, it makes 2 additional attacks with this weapon.
Klaive	Melee	Melee	+2	-3	2	-

WARGEAR OPTIONS

• The Klaivex's klaive can be replaced with 1 demiklaives.

ABILITIES

Blade Artists, Power From Pain (pg 89)

Lethal Precision: While this unit contains a Klaivex, each time a melee attack is made by a model in this unit, an unmodified wound roll of 6 adds 1 to the Damage characteristic of that attack.

Tormentors: At the start of the Fight phase, you can select one enemy unit within Engagement Range of this unit and roll 2D6: if the result is greater than the enemy unit's Leadership characteristic, that unit is not eligible to fight in the Fight phase until after all eligible units from your army have done so.

FACTION KEYWORDS: Aeldari, Drukhari
KEYWORDS: Infantry, Core, Blades for Hire, Incubi

The Incubi are warrior-perfectionists of the highest order. Protected by the ornate plates of their ancient warsuits, they move swiftly in for the kill, sweeping giant klaives in practised, decapitating strikes. They carve straight through the enemy's elite, crushing their spirit with psychic torture devices known as tormentors.

MANDRAKES

3 POWER

No.	Name	M	WS	BS	S	T	W	A	Ld	Sv
4-9	Mandrake	8"	3+	3+	4	3	1	3	7	7+
1	Nightfiend	8"	3+	3+	4	3	1	4	8	7+

If this unit contains 6 or more models, it has **Power Rating 6**. Every model is equipped with: baleblast; glimmersteel blade.

WEAPON	RANGE	TYPE	S	AP	D	ABILITIES
Baleblast	18"	Assault 2	4	-1	1	Each time an attack is made with this weapon, an unmodified wound roll of 6 inflicts 1 mortal wound on the target in addition to any normal damage.
Glimmersteel blade	Melee	Melee	User	-1	1	-

ABILITIES

Blade Artists, Power From Pain (pg 89)

From Out of the Shadows: During deployment, when you set up this unit, it can be set up anywhere on the battlefield that is more than 9" away from the enemy deployment zone and any enemy models.

Shrouded From Sight: Each time an attack targets this unit, subtract 1 from that attack's hit roll.

Shadow Creatures: Models in this unit have a 5+ invulnerable save.

Fade Away: Once per battle, at the start of your Movement phase, you can remove this unit from the battlefield and then, in the Reinforcements step of your next Movement phase, you can set this unit back up anywhere on the battlefield and more than 9" from any enemy models. If the battle ends and this unit is not on the battlefield, it is destroyed.

FACTION KEYWORDS: AELDARI, DRUKHARI
KEYWORDS: INFANTRY, BLADES FOR HIRE, MANDRAKES

Creatures of midnight horror, crawling from their shadow realm into the most secure locations, Mandrakes radiate an aura of frigid evil. Baleful runes carved into their shadowy flesh blaze with power, chilling their enemies' souls before these faceless reapers' icy blades and cold claws flense the skin from their victims.

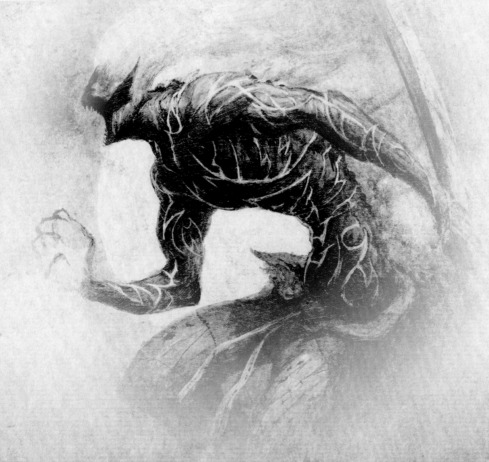

GROTESQUES

6 POWER

No.	Name	M	WS	BS	S	T	W	A	Ld	Sv
3-6	Grotesque	7"	3+	6+	5	5	4	4	8	6+

If this unit contains 4 or more models, it has **Power Rating 12**. Every model is equipped with: monstrous cleaver; flesh gauntlet.

WEAPON	RANGE	TYPE	S	AP	D	ABILITIES
Liquifier gun	12"	Assault D6	4	-2	1	Each time an attack is made with this weapon, that attack automatically hits the target.
Flesh gauntlet	Melee	Melee	+1	0	1	Each time an attack is made with this weapon, if the target is not a **VEHICLE** unit, an unmodified wound roll of 6 inflicts 1 mortal wound on the target in addition to any normal damage.
Monstrous cleaver	Melee	Melee	User	-2	2	Each time the bearer fights, it makes 1 additional attack with this weapon.

WARGEAR OPTIONS

- Any number of models can each have their monstrous cleaver replaced with 1 liquifier gun.

ABILITIES

Blade Artists, Insensible to Pain, Power From Pain (pg 89)

FACTION KEYWORDS: AELDARI, DRUKHARI, <HAEMONCULUS COVEN>
KEYWORDS: INFANTRY, CORE, GROTESQUES

These modified meat-hulks are pumped full of painful chemicals, growth elixirs and macro-steroids. With swollen muscles they hack their master's foes apart, their brutal cleavers and grafted claws dripping with toxins. They are mindlessly obedient and insensible to any hurt, chasing down fleeing prey at the behest of their creator.

BEASTMASTER

2 POWER

No.	Name	M	WS	BS	S	T	W	A	Ld	Sv
1	Beastmaster	12"	3+	3+	3	4	3	3	7	5+

A Beastmaster is equipped with: splinter pods; agoniser.

WEAPON	RANGE	TYPE	S	AP	D	ABILITIES
Splinter pods	18"	Assault 2	2	0	1	Poisoned Weapon (4+) (pg 89)
Agoniser	Melee	Melee	User	-3	1	Poisoned Weapon (4+) (pg 89)

ABILITIES

Blade Artists, Combat Drugs, Power From Pain (pg 89)

Beastmaster (Aura): While a friendly **Drukhari Beast** unit is within 6" of this model:
- Each time a model in that unit makes an attack, re-roll a hit roll of 1.
- Models in that unit can use this model's Leadership characteristic instead of their own.

Whips of the Master: In your Command phase, you can select one **Drukhari Beast** unit from your army that is within 6" of this model. That **Beast** unit is eligible to declare a charge this turn, even if it has Advanced.

Creature Handler: If your army is Battle-forged, then if a Detachment includes any **Drukhari Beast** units, one **Beastmaster** unit can be included in that Detachment without taking up a Battlefield Role slot.

FACTION KEYWORDS: Aeldari, Drukhari, <Wych Cult>
KEYWORDS: Infantry, Character, Skyboard, Fly, Beastmaster

On thrumming skyboards that spit venom-laced shards, Beastmasters hover above the frenzied bloodletting of their thrall-creatures, goading them on with the cruel lashes of a nerve-inflaming agoniser. Many wear shamanic masks that augment the wearer's natural dominance with sub-vocal emissions and subjugating pheromones.

CLAWED FIENDS

2 POWER

No.	Name	M	WS	BS	S	T	W	A	Ld	Sv
1-6	Clawed Fiend	10"	4+	-	5	5	4	5	4	5+

If this unit contains between 2 and 3 models, it has **Power Rating 5**. If this unit contains between 4 and 6 models, it has **Power Rating 10**. Every model is equipped with: clawed fists.

WEAPON	RANGE	TYPE	S	AP	D	ABILITIES
Clawed fists	Melee	Melee	User	-2	2	

ABILITIES

Beasts of the Arena: This unit can only be included in a Detachment if that Detachment also includes one or more **Drukhari Beastmaster** units, and you can only include a maximum of 3 **Drukhari Beast** units for each **Drukhari Beastmaster** unit in that Detachment.

Berserk Rage: While a model from this unit has lost any wounds, models in this unit have an Attacks characteristic of 6.

FACTION KEYWORDS: Aeldari, Drukhari
KEYWORDS: Beast, Blades for Hire, Clawed Fiends

Towering hulks of muscle, fur and razor-sharp talons, Clawed Fiends are monstrously fast with an array of hyper-advanced senses capable of locating their prey in multiple spectra. Though semi-sentient, they care for little save rending apart all in their path, entering a berserk fugue should their thick hide be pierced.

RAZORWING FLOCK

2 POWER

No.	Name	M	WS	BS	S	T	W	A	Ld	Sv
3-9	Razorwing Flock	12"	4+	-	2	2	4	4	4	7+

If this unit contains between 4 and 6 models, it has **Power Rating 4**. If this unit contains between 7 and 9 models, it has **Power Rating 6**. Every model is equipped with: razor feathers.

WEAPON	RANGE	TYPE	S	AP	D	ABILITIES
Razor feathers	Melee	Melee	User	-1	1	-

ABILITIES

Beasts of the Arena: This unit can only be included in a Detachment if that Detachment also includes one or more DRUKHARI BEASTMASTER units, and you can only include a maximum of 3 DRUKHARI BEAST units for each DRUKHARI BEASTMASTER unit in that Detachment.

FACTION KEYWORDS: AELDARI, DRUKHARI
KEYWORDS: BEAST, SWARM, FLY, BLADES FOR HIRE, RAZORWING FLOCKS

These bone-hungry raptors catch all but the swiftest of fleeing prey. Razorwings hunt in instinctive flocks, mobbing entire squads and tearing them apart with razor-edged wing tips and diamond-hard beaks. Stripping flesh from bone in moments, the Beastmaster's foes vanish in a whirlwind of blood and gore.

KHYMERAE

1 POWER

No.	Name	M	WS	BS	S	T	W	A	Ld	Sv
2-6	Khymerae	10"	3+	-	4	4	1	3	4	6+

If this unit contains between 3 and 4 models, it has **Power Rating 2**. If this unit contains between 5 and 6 models, it has **Power Rating 3**. Every model is equipped with: claws and talons.

WEAPON	RANGE	TYPE	S	AP	D	ABILITIES
Claws and talons	Melee	Melee	+1	-1	1	-

ABILITIES

Beasts of the Arena: This unit can only be included in a Detachment if that Detachment also includes one or more DRUKHARI BEASTMASTER units, and you can only include a maximum of 3 DRUKHARI BEAST units for each DRUKHARI BEASTMASTER unit in that Detachment.

Otherworldly: Models in this unit have a 5+ invulnerable save.

FACTION KEYWORDS: AELDARI, DRUKHARI
KEYWORDS: BEAST, DAEMON, BLADES FOR HIRE, KHYMERAE

Nightmare entities from daemon worlds, Khymerae are driven by the will of apex predators, appearing as skinned amalgams of claws, fangs and sinews. Loosed upon the Beastmaster's enemies, they wreak bloody havoc, tearing flesh apart with savage relish while their other-worldly nature defies the most powerful of blows.

REAVERS

No.	Name	M	WS	BS	S	T	W	A	Ld	Sv
2-11	Reaver	18"	3+	3+	3	4	2	3	7	4+
1	Arena Champion	18"	3+	3+	3	4	2	4	8	4+

If this unit contains between 4 and 6 models, it has **Power Rating 6**. If this unit contains between 7 and 9 models, it has **Power Rating 9**. If this unit contains between 9 and 12 models, it has **Power Rating 12**. Every model is equipped with: splinter pistol; splinter rifle; bladevanes.

WEAPON	RANGE	TYPE	S	AP	D	ABILITIES
Blaster	18"	Assault 1	8	-4	D6	-
Heat lance	18"	Heavy 1	8	-4	D6+2	-
Splinter pistol	12"	Pistol 1	2	0	1	Poisoned Weapon (4+) (pg 89)
Splinter rifle	24"	Rapid Fire 1	2	0	1	Poisoned Weapon (4+) (pg 89)
Agoniser	Melee	Melee	User	-3	1	Poisoned Weapon (4+) (pg 89)
Bladevanes	Melee	Melee	+1	-1	1	-
Power sword	Melee	Melee	+1	-3	1	-

OTHER WARGEAR	ABILITIES
Cluster caltrops	Each time an enemy unit within Engagement Range of the bearer Falls Back, roll one D6: on a 4+, that unit suffers 1 mortal wound.
Grav-talon	After the bearer makes a charge move, select one enemy unit within Engagement Range of them and roll one D6: on a 4+, that unit suffers 1 mortal wound. On a 6, that unit suffers D3 mortal wounds instead.

WARGEAR OPTIONS

- The Arena Champion can be equipped with one of the following: 1 power sword; 1 agoniser.
- For every 3 models in this unit, 1 model's splinter rifle can be replaced with one of the following: 1 blaster; 1 heat lance.
- For every 3 models in this unit, 1 model can be equipped with one of the following: 1 grav-talon; 1 cluster caltrops.

ABILITIES

Blade Artists, Combat Drugs, Power From Pain (pg 89)

Matchless Swiftness: Each time this unit Advances, do not make an Advance roll. Instead, until the end of the phase, add 8" to the Move characteristic of models in this unit.

FACTION KEYWORDS: AELDARI, DRUKHARI, <WYCH CULT>
KEYWORDS: BIKER, FLY, CORE, REAVERS

Reaver jetbikes streak across the battlefield with the same speed and agility they display during their lethal races around the Commorrite arenas. Whether jinking around incoming enemy fire, decapitating foes with vicious bladevanes or culling their victims with ferocious firepower, these high-speed killers are lethal in the extreme.

HELLIONS

4 POWER

No.	Name	M	WS	BS	S	T	W	A	Ld	Sv
4-19	Hellion	14"	3+	3+	3	4	2	3	7	5+
1	Helliarch	14"	3+	3+	3	4	2	4	8	5+

If this unit contains between 6 and 10 models, it has **Power Rating 7**. If this unit contains between 11 and 15 models, it has **Power Rating 11**. If this unit contains between 16 and 20 models, it has **Power Rating 15**. Every model is equipped with: splinter pods; hellglaive.

WEAPON	RANGE	TYPE	S	AP	D	ABILITIES
Phantasm grenade launcher	18"	Assault D3	-	-	-	Blast. Each time a unit is hit by this weapon, roll 2D6. If the result is higher than the Leadership characteristic of that unit, it suffers 1 mortal wound.
Splinter pistol	12"	Pistol 1	2	0	1	Poisoned Weapon (4+) (pg 89)
Splinter pods	18"	Assault 2	2	0	1	Poisoned Weapon (4+) (pg 89)
Agoniser	Melee	Melee	User	-3	1	Poisoned Weapon (4+) (pg 89)
Hellglaive	Melee	Melee	+1	-1	2	-
Power sword	Melee	Melee	+1	-3	1	-
Stunclaw	Melee	Melee	+1	0	2	Each time an attack is made with this weapon, an unmodified wound roll of 6 inflicts 1 mortal wound on the target in addition to any normal damage.

WARGEAR OPTIONS

- The Helliarch can be equipped with 1 phantasm grenade launcher.
- The Helliarch's hellglaive can be replaced with one of the following: 1 splinter pistol and 1 stunclaw; 1 splinter pistol and 1 power sword; 1 splinter pistol and 1 agoniser.

ABILITIES

Blade Artists, Combat Drugs, Power From Pain (pg 89)

Hit and Run: This unit is eligible to declare a charge in a turn in which it Fell Back.

FACTION KEYWORDS: **Aeldari, Drukhari, <Wych Cult>**
KEYWORDS: **Infantry, Skyboard, Fly, Core, Hellions**

When the Hellion gangs ride their bladed skyboards alongside Drukhari raiding parties, they bring terror to the battlefields of realspace. Arrogant and agile, Hellions wield their hellglaives with such skill that battle becomes a contest as to who can perform the most ostentatious acts of battlefield butchery.

SCOURGES

5 POWER

No.	Name	M	WS	BS	S	T	W	A	Ld	Sv
4-9	Scourge	14"	3+	3+	3	3	1	2	7	4+
1	Solarite	14"	3+	3+	3	3	1	3	8	4+

If this unit contains 6 or more models, it has **Power Rating 8**. Every model is equipped with: shardcarbine; plasma grenades.

WEAPON	RANGE	TYPE	S	AP	D	ABILITIES
Blast pistol	6"	Pistol 1	8	-4	D6	-
Blaster	18"	Assault 1	8	-4	D6	-
Dark lance	36"	Heavy 1	8	-4	D3+3	-
Drukhari haywire blaster	24"	Heavy D3	3	-3	D3	Blast. Each time an attack is made with this weapon, if the target is a **VEHICLE** unit, an unmodified wound roll of 4+ is always successful, and an unmodified wound roll of 6 inflicts D3 mortal wounds on the target in addition to any normal damage.
Heat lance	18"	Heavy 1	8	-4	D6+2	-
Shardcarbine	18"	Assault 3	2	0	1	Poisoned Weapon (4+) (pg 89)
Shredder	18"	Assault D6	6	-1	1	Blast
Splinter cannon	36"	Heavy 3	3	-1	2	Poisoned Weapon (4+) (pg 89)
Splinter pistol	12"	Pistol 1	2	0	1	Poisoned Weapon (4+) (pg 89)
Agoniser	Melee	Melee	User	-3	1	Poisoned Weapon (4+) (pg 89)
Power lance	Melee	Melee	+2	-2	1	-
Venom blade	Melee	Melee	User	-1	1	Poisoned Weapon (2+) (pg 89)
Plasma grenades	6"	Grenade D6	4	-1	1	Blast

WARGEAR OPTIONS

- Up to 4 Scourges can each have their shardcarbine replaced with one of the following: 1 blaster; 1 dark lance; 1 Drukhari haywire blaster; 1 heat lance; 1 shredder; 1 splinter cannon.
- The Solarite's shardcarbine can be replaced with one of the following: 1 splinter pistol; 1 blast pistol.
- The Solarite can be equipped with one of the following: 1 agoniser; 1 power lance; 1 venom blade.

ABILITIES

Blade Artists, Power From Pain (pg 89)

Ghostplate Armour: Models in this unit have a 5+ invulnerable save.

Winged Strike: During deployment, you can set up this unit high in the skies instead of setting it up on the battlefield. If you do so, then in the Reinforcements step of one of your Movement phases, you can set up this unit anywhere on the battlefield that is more than 9" away from any enemy models.

FACTION KEYWORDS: **AELDARI, DRUKHARI**
KEYWORDS: **INFANTRY, FLY, HAYWIRE GRENADE, CORE, BLADES FOR HIRE, SCOURGES**

Airborne messengers and mercenaries who ride the thermals between Commorragh's highest spires, Scourges have been bodily modified for winged flight. They wear their grotesque new forms with the same pride that they wield their massive dark lances and splinter cannons, for their combination of speed and firepower renders them invaluable.

TALOS

No.	Name	M	WS	BS	S	T	W	A	Ld	Sv
1-3	Talos	8"	3+	4+	6	6	7	5	8	3+

If this unit contains 2 models, it has **Power Rating 12**. If this unit contains 3 models, it has **Power Rating 18**. Every model is equipped with: 2 splinter cannons; 2 macro-scalpels.

WEAPON	RANGE	TYPE	S	AP	D	ABILITIES
Drukhari haywire blaster	24"	Heavy D3	3	-3	D3	Blast. Each time an attack is made with this weapon, if the target is a **VEHICLE** unit, an unmodified wound roll of 4+ is always successful, and an unmodified wound roll of 6 inflicts D3 mortal wounds on the target in addition to any normal damage.
Heat lance	18"	Heavy 1	8	-4	D6+2	-
Splinter cannon	36"	Heavy 3	3	-1	2	Poisoned Weapon (4+) (pg 89)
Stinger pod	24"	Assault 2D6	5	0	1	-
Twin liquifier gun	12"	Assault 2D6	4	-2	1	Each time an attack is made with this weapon, that attack automatically hits the target.
Chain-flails	Melee	Melee	User	0	1	Each time an attack is made with this weapon, make 2 hit rolls instead of 1.
Macro-scalpel	Melee	Melee	+1	-2	2	Each time the bearer fights, if it is equipped with 2 macro-scalpels, it makes 1 additional attack with this weapon.
Talos ichor injector	Melee	Melee	-	-	-	Each time the bearer fights, no more than one attack can be made with this weapon. Each time an attack is made with this weapon, if a hit is scored, the target suffers D3 mortal wounds and the attack sequence ends.
Talos gauntlet	Melee	Melee	+2	-3	3	Each time an attack is made with this weapon, subtract 1 from that attack's hit roll.

WARGEAR OPTIONS

- Any number of models can each have one of their macro-scalpels replaced with one of the following: 1 Talos ichor injector; 1 twin liquifier gun.
- Any number of models can each have one of their macro-scalpels replaced with one of the following: 1 chain-flails; 1 Talos gauntlet.
- Any number of models can each have their 2 splinter cannons replaced with one of the following: 2 Drukhari haywire blasters; 2 heat lances; 1 stinger pod.

ABILITIES

Blade Artists, Insensible To Pain, Power From Pain (pg 89)

Explodes: Each time a model in this unit is destroyed, roll one D6 before removing it from play. On a 6 it explodes, and each unit within 3" suffers 1 mortal wound.

FACTION KEYWORDS: **AELDARI, DRUKHARI, <HAEMONCULUS COVEN>**
KEYWORDS: **MONSTER, CORE, FLY, TALOS**

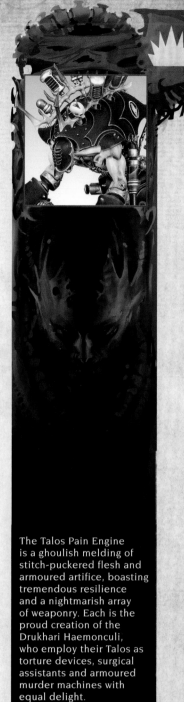

The Talos Pain Engine is a ghoulish melding of stitch-puckered flesh and armoured artifice, boasting tremendous resilience and a nightmarish array of weaponry. Each is the proud creation of the Drukhari Haemonculi, who employ their Talos as torture devices, surgical assistants and armoured murder machines with equal delight.

CRONOS

No.	Name	M	WS	BS	S	T	W	A	Ld	Sv
1-3	Cronos	8"	4+	3+	5	6	7	4	9	3+

If this unit contains 2 models, it has **Power Rating 8**. If this unit contains 3 models, it has **Power Rating 12**. Every model is equipped with: spirit syphon; spirit-leech tentacles.

WEAPON	RANGE	TYPE	S	AP	D	ABILITIES
Spirit syphon	12"	Assault D6	5	-2	1	Each time an attack is made with this weapon, that attack automatically hits the target. Each time an attack is made with this weapon, on an unmodified wound roll of 6, that attack has a Damage characteristic of 2.
Spirit vortex	18"	Assault D6	5	-2	1	Blast. Each time an attack is made with this weapon, on an unmodified wound roll of 6, that attack has a Damage characteristic of 2.
Spirit-leech tentacles	Melee	Melee	User	-1	1	Each time an attack is made with this weapon, on an unmodified wound roll of 6, that attack has a Damage characteristic of 2.

OTHER WARGEAR	ABILITIES
Spirit probe	The bearer gains the following ability: '**Spirit Probe (Aura):** While a friendly **DRUKHARI CORE** or **DRUKHARI CHARACTER** unit is within 6" of the bearer, each time a model in that unit makes a melee attack, you can re-roll a wound roll of 1.'

WARGEAR OPTIONS

- Any number of models can each be equipped with 1 spirit vortex.
- Any number of models can each be equipped with 1 spirit probe.

ABILITIES

Blade Artists, Insensible To Pain, Power From Pain (pg 89)

Explodes: Each time a model in this unit is destroyed, roll one D6 before removing it from play. On a 6 it explodes, and each unit within 3" suffers 1 mortal wound.

Reservoir of Pain: Each time a model in this unit destroys an enemy model with its spirit-leech tentacles, you can select this unit or one other **DRUKHARI CORE** unit within 6" of this unit. After this unit has fought, one model in the selected unit regains 1 lost wound (if no models in that unit have lost any wounds, but the unit is not at its Starting Strength, you can instead return 1 destroyed model to that unit with one wound remaining – this model can be set up in Engagement Range of an enemy unit that is already in Engagement Range of the unit it is being returned to).

FACTION KEYWORDS: AELDARI, DRUKHARI, <HAEMONCULUS COVEN>
KEYWORDS: MONSTER, CORE, FLY, CRONOS

Like other Engines of Pain, the Cronos is a grisly amalgam of stimm-fed flesh and biomechanical implements shielded by a burnished carapace. Haemonculi create the Cronos to act as a parasite. Its esoteric syphons leech its victim's life essence, leaving them as husks before projecting the stolen vitality to other Drukhari.

'When I look upon the lesser races, I am filled with disgust. Left to their own devices, they lead lives that are pitifully brief and completely devoid of meaning. How many of their generations have passed by in my lifetime? The answer is beneath my attention. Yet with the correct application of my art, each of those wretched beings can be made to endure an eternity of suffering, and it is through their screams that they show me their value.'

- Urien Rakarth, Master Haemonculus of the Prophets of Flesh

RAVAGER

8 POWER

Some of this model's characteristics change as it suffers damage, as shown below:

No.	Name	M	WS	BS	S	T	W	A	Ld	Sv
1	Ravager (6+ wounds remaining)	14"	4+	3+	6	6	11	3	7	4+
	Ravager (3-5 wounds remaining)	10"	4+	4+	6	6	N/A	D3	7	4+
	Ravager (1-2 wounds remaining)	6"	4+	5+	6	6	N/A	1	7	4+

A Ravager is equipped with: 3 dark lances; bladevanes.

WEAPON	RANGE	TYPE	S	AP	D	ABILITIES
Dark lance	36"	Heavy 1	8	-4	D3+3	-
Disintegrator cannon	36"	Heavy 3	5	-3	2	-
Phantasm grenade launcher	18"	Assault D3	-	-	-	Blast. Each time a unit is hit by this weapon, roll 2D6. If the result is higher than the Leadership characteristic of that unit, it suffers 1 mortal wound.
Bladevanes	Melee	Melee	+1	-1	1	-

OTHER WARGEAR	ABILITIES
Chain-snares	Add 3 to the bearer's Attacks characteristic.
Grisly trophies	The bearer gains the following ability: 'Grisly Trophies (Aura): While an enemy unit is within 3" of this model, subtract 2 from the Leadership characteristic of models in that unit.'
Shock prow	The bearer has the **SHOCK PROW** keyword.

WARGEAR OPTIONS

- This model's dark lances can each be replaced with 1 disintegrator cannon.
- This model can be equipped with any of the following: 1 chain-snares; 1 grisly trophies; 1 phantasm grenade launcher; 1 shock prow.

ABILITIES

Blade Artists, Power From Pain (pg 89)

Night Shield: This model has a 5+ invulnerable save against ranged attacks.

Hovering: Distances are always measured to and from this model's hull.

Explodes: When this model is destroyed, roll one D6 before removing it from play. On a 6 it explodes, and each unit within 6" suffers D3 mortal wounds.

FACTION KEYWORDS: **AELDARI, DRUKHARI, <KABAL>**
KEYWORDS: **VEHICLE, FLY, RAVAGER**

Ravager gunships fulfil the role of armoured support during Drukhari raids, yet these grav-skiffs also possess the speed and agility to outmanoeuvre the enemy's lumbering equivalents. They are mobile assassins, mounting enough firepower to gut enemy tanks and eradicate the foe's elite, before swiftly moving to new hunting grounds.

RAIDER

5 POWER

Some of this model's characteristics change as it suffers damage, as shown below:

No.	Name	M	WS	BS	S	T	W	A	Ld	Sv
1	Raider (6+ wounds remaining)	14"	4+	3+	6	6	10	3	7	4+
	Raider (3-5 wounds remaining)	10"	4+	4+	6	6	N/A	D3	7	4+
	Raider (1-2 wounds remaining)	6"	4+	5+	6	6	N/A	1	7	4+

A Raider is equipped with: dark lance; bladevanes.

WEAPON	RANGE	TYPE	S	AP	D	ABILITIES
Dark lance	36"	Heavy 1	8	-4	D3+3	-
Disintegrator cannon	36"	Heavy 3	5	-3	2	-
Phantasm grenade launcher	18"	Assault D3	-	-	-	Blast. Each time a unit is hit by this weapon, roll 2D6. If the result is higher than the Leadership characteristic of that unit, it suffers 1 mortal wound.
Bladevanes	Melee	Melee	+1	-1	1	-

OTHER WARGEAR	ABILITIES
Chain-snares	Add 3 to the bearer's Attacks characteristic.
Grisly trophies	The bearer gains the following ability: '**Grisly Trophies (Aura):** While an enemy unit is within 3" of this model, subtract 2 from the Leadership characteristic of models in that unit.'
Shock prow	The bearer has the **SHOCK PROW** keyword.
Splinter racks	Each time a model embarked on this transport makes an attack with a Rapid Fire weapon, treat the target as being within half that weapon's range.

WARGEAR OPTIONS

- This model's dark lance can be replaced with 1 disintegrator cannon.
- This model can be equipped with any of the following: 1 chain-snares; 1 grisly trophies; 1 phantasm grenade launcher; 1 shock prow; 1 splinter racks.

ABILITIES

Blade Artists, Power From Pain (pg 89)

Open-topped: In your Shooting phase, units embarked within this transport can be selected to shoot with; measure distances and draw line of sight from any point on this transport when doing so. If this transport made a Normal Move, Advanced or Fell Back this turn, embarked units are considered to have done the same. While this transport is within Engagement Range of any enemy units, embarked units cannot shoot, except with Pistols.

Hovering: Distances are always measured to and from this model's hull.

Night Shield: This model has a 5+ invulnerable save against ranged attacks.

Explodes: When this transport is destroyed, roll one D6 before any embarked models disembark and before removing it from play. On a 6 it explodes, and each unit within 6" suffers D3 mortal wounds.

TRANSPORT

This model has a transport capacity of 11 **DRUKHARI INFANTRY** models. Each **GROTESQUES** model takes the space of two models. This model cannot transport **SCOURGES** or **SKYBOARD** models.

FACTION KEYWORDS: **AELDARI, DRUKHARI, <HAEMONCULUS COVEN>** OR **<KABAL>** OR **<WYCH CULT>**
KEYWORDS: **VEHICLE, TRANSPORT, FLY, RAIDER**

The Raider is a favoured transport cutter among the Drukhari. Its passengers loose shots from the trophy-hung decking as it speeds upon anti-grav turbines into the fighting. While its cargo of warriors leaps into the fray, the Raider unleashes its heavy weaponry and flays enemies below with chain-snares and bladevanes.

VENOM

4 POWER

No.	Name	M	WS	BS	S	T	W	A	Ld	Sv
1	Venom	16"	4+	3+	5	5	6	3	7	4+

A Venom is equipped with: splinter cannon; twin splinter rifle; bladevanes.

WEAPON	RANGE	TYPE	S	AP	D	ABILITIES
Splinter cannon	36"	Heavy 3	3	-1	2	Poisoned Weapon (4+) (pg 89)
Twin splinter rifle	24"	Rapid Fire 2	2	0	1	Poisoned Weapon (4+) (pg 89)
Bladevanes	Melee	Melee	+1	-1	1	-

OTHER WARGEAR	ABILITIES
Chain-snares	Add 3 to the bearer's Attacks characteristic.
Grisly trophies	The bearer gains the following ability: 'Grisly Trophies (Aura): While an enemy unit is within 3" of this model, subtract 2 from the Leadership characteristic of models in that unit.'

WARGEAR OPTIONS

- This model's twin splinter rifle can be replaced with 1 splinter cannon.
- This model can be equipped with any of the following: 1 chain-snares; 1 grisly trophies.

ABILITIES

Blade Artists, Power From Pain (pg 89)

Open-topped: In your Shooting phase, units embarked within this transport can be selected to shoot with; measure distances and draw line of sight from any point on this transport when doing so. If this transport made a Normal Move, Advanced or Fell Back this turn, embarked units are considered to have done the same. While this transport is within Engagement Range of any enemy units, embarked units cannot shoot, except with Pistols.

Flickerfield: Each time a ranged attack is made against this model, subtract 1 from that attack's hit roll. This model has a 5+ invulnerable save against ranged attacks.

Hovering: Distances are always measured to and from this model's hull.

Explodes: When this transport is destroyed, roll one D6 before any embarked models disembark and before removing it from play. On a 6 it explodes, and each unit within 6" suffers 1 mortal wound.

TRANSPORT

This model has a transport capacity of 6 DRUKHARI INFANTRY models. This model cannot transport GROTESQUES, SCOURGES or SKYBOARD models.

FACTION KEYWORDS: **AELDARI, DRUKHARI, <HAEMONCULUS COVEN> OR <KABAL> OR <WYCH CULT>**
KEYWORDS: **VEHICLE, TRANSPORT, FLY, VENOM**

Raw speed delivers countless light Venom transports to the heart of the enemy's defence, and sees them chase down stragglers and encircle the foe's outriders. For the clique of warriors on board, Venoms are mobile firebases and gore-splashed chariots in one, with flickering shields that confound attempts to bring them down.

RAZORWING JETFIGHTER

8 POWER

Some of this model's characteristics change as it suffers damage, as shown below:

No.	Name	M	WS	BS	S	T	W	A	Ld	Sv
1	Razorwing Jetfighter (6+ wounds remaining)	20-72"	6+	3+	6	6	10	3	7	4+
	Razorwing Jetfighter (3-5 wounds remaining)	20-48"	6+	4+	6	6	N/A	D3	7	4+
	Razorwing Jetfighter (1-2 wounds remaining)	20-32"	6+	5+	6	6	N/A	1	7	4+

A Razorwing Jetfighter is equipped with: 2 dark lances; Razorwing missiles; twin splinter rifle.

WEAPON	RANGE	TYPE	S	AP	D	ABILITIES
Dark lance	36"	Heavy 1	8	-4	D3+3	-
Disintegrator cannon	36"	Heavy 3	5	-3	2	-
Razorwing missiles	Before selecting targets, select one of the profiles below to make attacks with.					
- Monoscythe missile	48"	Assault D6	6	0	2	Blast
- Necrotoxin missile	48"	Assault 3D3	2	0	1	Blast. Poisoned Weapon (2+) (pg 89)
- Shatterfield missile	48"	Assault D6	7	-2	1	Blast
Splinter cannon	36"	Heavy 3	3	-1	2	Poisoned Weapon (4+) (pg 89)
Twin splinter rifle	24"	Rapid Fire 2	2	0	1	Poisoned Weapon (4+) (pg 89)

WARGEAR OPTIONS

- This model's 2 dark lances can be replaced with 2 disintegrator cannons.
- This model's twin splinter rifle can be replaced with 1 splinter cannon.

ABILITIES

Power From Pain (pg 89)

Supersonic: Each time this model makes a Normal Move, Advances or Falls Back, first pivot it on the spot up to 90° (this does not contribute to how far the model moves), then move the model straight forwards. It cannot pivot again after the initial pivot.

Night Shield: This model has a 5+ invulnerable save against ranged attacks.

Hard to Hit: Each time a ranged attack is made against this model, subtract 1 from that attack's hit roll.

Airborne: You cannot declare a charge with this model, and it can only be chosen as a target of a charge if the unit making the charge can **FLY**. You can only fight with this model if it is within Engagement Range of any enemy units that can **FLY**, and this model can only make melee attacks against units that can **FLY**. Enemy units can only make melee attacks against this model if they can **FLY**.

Explodes: When this model is destroyed, roll one D6 before removing it from play. On a 6 it explodes, and each unit within 6" suffers D3 mortal wounds.

FACTION KEYWORDS: **Aeldari, Drukhari, <Kabal>** OR **<Wych Cult>**
KEYWORDS: **Vehicle, Fly, Aircraft, Razorwing Jetfighter**

These lightning-fast ground attack craft unleash widespread slaughter and disruption with flurries of morbidly diverse missiles. Archons call in their strikes to fracture the lesser races' attempts at organised resistance, and their speed-addicted pilots also indulge in hunting down lumbering tanks and monstrosities with multiple heavy cannons.

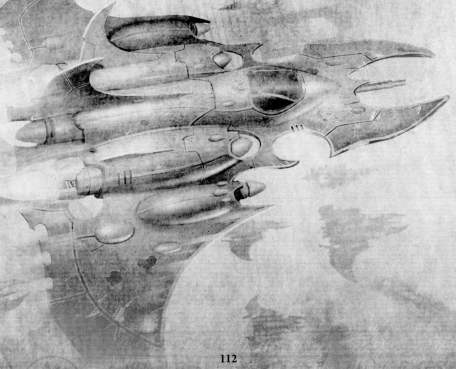

VOIDRAVEN BOMBER

Some of this model's characteristics change as it suffers damage, as shown below:

No.	Name	M	WS	BS	S	T	W	A	Ld	Sv
1	Voidraven Bomber (7+ wounds remaining)	20-60"	6+	3+	6	6	12	3	7	4+
	Voidraven Bomber (4-6 wounds remaining)	20-40"	6+	4+	6	6	N/A	D3	7	4+
	Voidraven Bomber (1-3 wounds remaining)	20-25"	6+	5+	6	6	N/A	1	7	4+

A Voidraven Bomber is equipped with: 2 void lances; void mine.

WEAPON	RANGE	TYPE	S	AP	D	ABILITIES
Dark scythe	24"	Heavy 3	8	-4	2	-
Void lance	36"	Heavy 1	9	-4	D3+3	-
Voidraven missiles	Before selecting targets, select one of the profiles below to make attacks with.					
- Implosion missile	48"	Assault D3	6	-3	2	Blast
- Shatterfield missile	48"	Assault D6	7	-2	1	Blast

OTHER WARGEAR	ABILITIES
Void mine	Once per battle, in your Movement phase, after the bearer makes a Normal Move or Advances, you can select one point on the battlefield the bearer moved across. Roll one D6 for each unit within 6" of that point, subtracting 1 if that unit has the **CHARACTER** keyword (excluding **VEHICLE** or **MONSTER** units): on a 4+, that unit suffers D6 mortal wounds.

WARGEAR OPTIONS

- This model's 2 void lances can be replaced with 2 dark scythes.
- This model can be equipped with Voidraven missiles.

ABILITIES

Power From Pain (pg 89)

Supersonic: Each time this model makes a Normal Move, Advances or Falls Back, first pivot it on the spot up to 90° (this does not contribute to how far the model moves), then move the model straight forwards. It cannot pivot again after the initial pivot.

Night Shield: This model has a 5+ invulnerable save against ranged attacks.

Hard to Hit: Each time a ranged attack is made against this model, subtract 1 from that attack's hit roll.

Airborne: You cannot declare a charge with this model, and it can only be chosen as a target of a charge if the unit making the charge can **FLY**. You can only fight with this model if it is within Engagement Range of any enemy units that can **FLY**, and this model can only make melee attacks against units that can **FLY**. Enemy units can only make melee attacks against this model if they can **FLY**.

Explodes: When this model is destroyed, roll one D6 before removing it from play. On a 6 it explodes, and each unit within 6" suffers D3 mortal wounds.

FACTION KEYWORDS: **AELDARI, DRUKHARI, <KABAL>** OR **<WYCH CULT>**
KEYWORDS: **VEHICLE, FLY, AIRCRAFT, VOIDRAVEN BOMBER**

Mounting some of the most powerful guns in the Drukhari arsenal, the Voidraven Bomber's dark scythes and void lances can crack fortifications and heavily armoured targets. Yet they pale against the silent aircraft's primary weapon – the void mine. Once this arcane payload is deployed, the resulting darklight implosion erases all caught within its blast.

POINTS VALUES

You can use this section to determine the points (pts) value of each unit in your army. Each entry lists the unit's size (i.e. how many models the unit can contain) and how many points the unit costs. If an entry has a unit cost of '*x* pts/model', then the unit costs *x* points for every model in that unit. You must then add points for each weapon, or other item of wargear, that is included in that unit if it is listed in that unit's entry (weapons and other wargear not listed in a unit's entry cost no additional points to include in that unit).

☠ HQ

Archon (pg 90)
Unit size .... 1 model
Unit cost .... 65 pts
- Blast pistol .... +5 pts
- Huskblade .... +5 pts

Drazhar (pg 93)
Unit size .... 1 model
Unit cost .... 135 pts

Haemonculus (pg 91)
Unit size .... 1 model
Unit cost .... 80 pts

Lelith Hesperax (pg 92)
Unit size .... 1 model
Unit cost .... 90 pts

Succubus (pg 91)
Unit size .... 1 model
Unit cost .... 60 pts

Urien Rakarth (pg 94)
Unit size .... 1 model
Unit cost .... 100 pts

▶ TROOPS

Kabalite Warriors (pg 95)
Unit size 5-20
Unit cost .... 8 pts/model
- Agoniser .... +5 pts
- Blast pistol .... +5 pts
- Blaster .... +10 pts
- Dark lance .... +15 pts
- Phantasm grenade launcher .... +5 pts
- Power sword .... +5 pts
- Shredder .... +5 pts
- Splinter cannon .... +10 pts

Wyches (pg 96)
Unit size 5-20
Unit cost .... 10 pts/model
- Agoniser .... +5 pts
- Blast pistol .... +5 pts
- Hydra gauntlets .... +5 pts
- Phantasm grenade launcher .... +5 pts
- Power sword .... +5 pts
- Razorflails .... +5 pts
- Shardnet and impaler .... +10 pts

Wracks (pg 97)
Unit size 5-20
Unit cost .... 8 pts/model
- Agoniser .... +5 pts
- Electrocorrosive whip .... +5 pts
- Flesh gauntlet .... +5 pts
- Hexrifle .... +5 pts
- Liquifier gun .... +10 pts
- Mindphase gauntlet .... +5 pts
- Ossefactor .... +5 pts
- Scissorhand .... +10 pts
- Stinger pistol .... +5 pts
- Venom blade .... +5 pts

✦ ELITES

Beastmaster (pg 102)
Unit size .... 1 model
Unit cost .... 40 pts

Court of the Archon (pg 98)
Unit size 4-16
Unit cost ....
- Lhamaean .... 16 pts/model
- Medusae .... 22 pts/model
- Sslyth .... 18 pts/model
- Ur-Ghul .... 16 pts/model

Grotesques (pg 101)
Unit size 3-6
Unit cost .... 40 pts/model
- Liquifier gun .... +5 pts

Incubi (pg 99)
Unit size 5-10
Unit cost .... 16 pts/model

Mandrakes (pg 100)
Unit size 5-10
Unit cost .... 15 pts/model

'The galaxy's battlefields provide almost as great a thrill as the arenas, but some adaptations are necessary. Without a proper audience, I must slice the eyelids off my victims so that I know they are witnessing the true extent of my skill. When I am finished, I must make do with the wet applause that comes from the flapping of their rent flesh.'

- Resputia the Razor, Wych of the Red Grief

⚡ FAST ATTACK

Clawed Fiends (pg 102)
Unit size 1-6
Unit cost .... 25 pts/model

Hellions (pg 105)
Unit size 5-20
Unit cost .... 17 pts/model
- Agoniser .... +5 pts
- Phantasm grenade launcher .... +5 pts
- Power sword .... +5 pts
- Stunclaw .... +5 pts

Khymerae (pg 103)
Unit size 2-6
Unit cost .... 10 pts/model

Razorwing Flock (pg 103)
Unit size 3-9
Unit cost .... 12 pts/model

Reavers (pg 104)
Unit size 3-12
Unit cost .... 10 pts/model
- Agoniser .... +5 pts
- Blaster .... +15 pts
- Cluster caltrops .... +5 pts
- Grav-talon .... +5 pts
- Heat lance .... +10 pts
- Power sword .... +5 pts

Scourges (pg 106)
Unit size 5-10
Unit cost .... 12 pts/model
- Agoniser .... +5 pts
- Blast pistol .... +5 pts
- Blaster .... +10 pts
- Dark lance .... +15 pts
- Drukhari haywire blaster .... +10 pts
- Heat lance .... +10 pts
- Shredder .... +5 pts
- Splinter cannon .... +10 pts
- Power lance .... +5 pts
- Venom blade .... +5 pts

👑 HEAVY SUPPORT

Cronos (pg 108)
Unit size 1-3
Unit cost .... 70 pts/model
- Spirit probe .... +5 pts
- Spirit vortex .... +10 pts

Ravager (pg 109)
Unit size .... 1 model
Unit cost .... 140 pts
- Chain-snares .... +5 pts
- Disintegrator cannon .... +5 pts
- Grisly trophies .... +5 pts
- Phantasm grenade launcher .... +5 pts
- Shock prow .... +5 pts

Talos (pg 107)
Unit size 1-3
Unit cost .... 110 pts/model
- Talos gauntlet .... +5 pts
- Twin liquifier gun .... +15 pts

💀 DEDICATED TRANSPORTS

Raider (pg 110)
Unit size .... 1 model
Unit cost .... 85 pts
- Chain-snares .... +5 pts
- Disintegrator cannon .... +5 pts
- Grisly trophies .... +5 pts
- Phantasm grenade launcher .... +5 pts
- Shock prow .... +5 pts
- Splinter racks .... +10 pts

Venom (pg 111)
Unit size .... 1 model
Unit cost .... 65 pts
- Chain-snares .... +5 pts
- Grisly trophies .... +5 pts
- Splinter cannon .... +10 pts

🌿 FLYERS

Razorwing Jetfighter (pg 112)
Unit size .... 1 model
Unit cost .... 160 pts
- Disintegrator cannon .... +5 pts
- Splinter cannon .... +5 pts

Voidraven Bomber (pg 113)
Unit size .... 1 model
Unit cost .... 185 pts
- Dark scythe .... +5 pts
- Voidraven missiles .... +15 pts

WEAPON PROFILES

Below you will find the profiles for all the weapons that Drukhari models can be equipped with. Note that some weapons have the Blast ability; this ability is detailed in full in the Warhammer 40,000 Core Book.

WEAPON DEFINITIONS

Some rules refer to 'splinter weapons' or 'Wych weapons'. The definitions of these weapons for the purposes of such rules can be found below:

Splinter Weapons

A splinter weapon is a shardcarbine or any weapon whose profile includes the word 'splinter' (splinter rifle, splinter cannon, splinter pods etc.), and any Relic that replaces a splinter weapon (e.g. Parasite's Kiss, page 74).

Wych Weapons

'Wych weapons' is a catch-all term for the traditional ritual weapons used by Wyches in their arena performances. The following weapons are Wych weapons:

- Archite glaive
- Hekatarii blade
- Hydra gauntlets
- Razorflails
- Shardnet and impaler

Any Relic that replaces one of these weapons (e.g. Dancer's Edge, page 51) is also considered to be a Wych weapon.

RANGED WEAPONS	RANGE	TYPE	S	AP	D	ABILITIES
Baleblast	18"	Assault 2	4	-1	1	Each time an attack is made with this weapon, an unmodified wound roll of 6 inflicts 1 mortal wound on the target in addition to any normal damage.
Blast pistol	6"	Pistol 1	8	-4	D6	-
Blaster	18"	Assault 1	8	-4	D6	-
Casket of Flensing	12"	Assault 2D6	3	-2	1	The bearer can only shoot with this weapon once per battle. Each time an attack is made with this weapon, that attack automatically hits the target.
Dark lance	36"	Heavy 1	8	-4	D3+3	-
Dark scythe	24"	Heavy 3	8	-4	2	-
Disintegrator cannon	36"	Heavy 3	5	-3	2	-
Eyeburst	12"	Pistol D6	4	-2	1	Each time an attack is made with this weapon, that attack automatically hits the target.
Drukhari haywire blaster	24"	Heavy D3	3	-3	D3	Blast. Each time an attack is made with this weapon, if the target is a VEHICLE unit, an unmodified wound roll of 4+ is always successful, and an unmodified wound roll of 6 inflicts D3 mortal wounds on the target in addition to any normal damage.
Heat lance	18"	Heavy 1	8	-4	D6+2	-
Hexrifle	36"	Heavy 1	6	-2	2	Each time you select a target for this weapon, you can ignore the Look Out, Sir rule. Each time an attack is made with this weapon, an unmodified wound roll of 6 inflicts 1 mortal wound on the target in addition to any normal damage.
Liquifier gun	12"	Assault D6	4	-2	1	Each time an attack is made with this weapon, that attack automatically hits the target.
Ossefactor	24"	Assault 1	2	-3	2	Poisoned Weapon (2+) (pg 89)
Phantasm grenade launcher	18"	Assault D3	-	-	-	Blast. Each time a unit is hit by this weapon, roll 2D6. If the result is higher than the Leadership characteristic of that unit, it suffers 1 mortal wound.
Plasma grenades	6"	Grenade D6	4	-1	1	Blast
Razorwing missiles	Before selecting targets, select one of the profiles below to make attacks with.					
- Monoscythe missile	48"	Assault D6	6	0	2	Blast
- Necrotoxin missile	48"	Assault 3D3	2	0	1	Blast. Poisoned Weapon (2+) (pg 89)
- Shatterfield missile	48"	Assault D6	7	-2	1	Blast
Shardcarbine	18"	Assault 3	2	0	1	Poisoned Weapon (4+) (pg 89)
Shredder	18"	Assault D6	6	-1	1	Blast
Spirit syphon	12"	Assault D6	5	-2	1	Each time an attack is made with this weapon, that attack automatically hits the target. Each time an attack is made with this weapon, on an unmodified wound roll of 6, that attack has a Damage characteristic of 2.
Spirit vortex	18"	Assault D6	5	-2	1	Blast. Each time an attack is made with this weapon, on an unmodified wound roll of 6, that attack has a Damage characteristic of 2.
Splinter cannon	36"	Heavy 3	3	-1	2	Poisoned Weapon (4+) (pg 89)

116

RANGED WEAPONS	RANGE	TYPE	S	AP	D	ABILITIES
Splinter pistol	12"	Pistol 1	2	0	1	Poisoned Weapon (4+) (pg 89)
Splinter pods	18"	Assault 2	2	0	1	Poisoned Weapon (4+) (pg 89)
Splinter rifle	24"	Rapid Fire 1	2	0	1	Poisoned Weapon (4+) (pg 89)
Stinger pistol	12"	Pistol 1	2	0	1	Poisoned Weapon (2+) (pg 89)
Stinger pod	24"	Assault 2D6	5	0	1	-
Twin liquifier gun	12"	Assault 2D6	4	-2	1	Each time an attack is made with this weapon, that attack automatically hits the target.
Twin splinter rifle	24"	Rapid Fire 2	2	0	1	Poisoned Weapon (4+) (pg 89)
Void lance	36"	Heavy 1	9	-4	D3+3	-
Voidraven missiles	Before selecting targets, select one of the profiles below to make attacks with.					
- Implosion missile	48"	Assault D3	6	-3	2	Blast
- Shatterfield missile	48"	Assault D6	7	-2	1	Blast

MELEE WEAPONS	RANGE	TYPE	S	AP	D	ABILITIES
Agoniser	Melee	Melee	User	-3	1	Poisoned Weapon (4+) (pg 89)
Archite glaive	Melee	Melee	+2	-3	1	-
Bladevanes	Melee	Melee	+1	-1	1	-
Chain-flails	Melee	Melee	User	0	1	Each time an attack is made with this weapon, make 2 hit rolls instead of 1.
Clawed fists	Melee	Melee	User	-2	2	-
Claws and talons	Melee	Melee	+1	-1	1	-
Demiklaives	Before selecting targets, select one of the profiles below to make attacks with.					
- Single blade	Melee	Melee	+2	-3	2	-
- Dual blades	Melee	Melee	+1	-2	2	Each time the bearer fights, if this weapon profile is selected, it makes 2 additional attacks with this weapon.
Electrocorrosive whip	Melee	Melee	2	-2	1	Poisoned Weapon (4+) (pg 89). Each time an attack is made with this weapon, make 2 hit rolls instead of 1.
The Executioner's demiklaives	Before selecting targets, select one of the profiles below to make attacks with.					
- Single blade	Melee	Melee	+2	-3	3	-
- Dual blades	Melee	Melee	+1	-3	2	Each time the bearer fights, if this weapon profile is selected, it makes 2 additional attacks with this weapon.
Flesh gauntlet	Melee	Melee	+1	0	1	Each time an attack is made with this weapon, if the target is not a VEHICLE unit, an unmodified wound roll of 6 inflicts 1 mortal wound on the target in addition to any normal damage.
Glimmersteel blade	Melee	Melee	User	-1	1	-
Haemonculus tools	Melee	Melee	User	0	1	Poisoned Weapon (2+) (pg 89)
Hekatarii blade	Melee	Melee	User	-1	1	Each time the bearer fights, it makes 1 additional attack with this weapon.
Hellglaive	Melee	Melee	+1	-1	2	-
Huskblade	Melee	Melee	User	-2	2	-
Hydra gauntlets	Melee	Melee	+2	-2	1	Each time the bearer fights, it makes 1 additional attack with this weapon.
Ichor injector	Melee	Melee	-	-	-	Each time the bearer fights, no more than one attack can be made with this weapon. Each time an attack is made with this weapon, if a hit is scored, the target suffers 1 mortal wound and the attack sequence ends.
Klaive	Melee	Melee	+2	-3	2	-
Lelith's blades	Melee	Melee	+1	-3	1	Each time an attack is made with this weapon, an unmodified hit roll of 6 scores 1 additional hit.
Macro-scalpel	Melee	Melee	+1	-2	2	Each time the bearer fights, if it is equipped with 2 macro-scalpels, it makes 1 additional attack with this weapon.
Mindphase gauntlet	Melee	Melee	User	-1	2	-
Monstrous cleaver	Melee	Melee	User	-2	2	Each time the bearer fights, it makes 1 additional attack with this weapon.
Power lance	Melee	Melee	+2	-2	1	-
Power sword	Melee	Melee	+1	-3	1	-
Razor feathers	Melee	Melee	User	-1	1	-
Razorflails	Melee	Melee	User	-1	1	Each time an attack is made with this weapon, make 2 hit rolls instead of 1.
Scissorhand	Melee	Melee	User	-2	1	Poisoned Weapon (4+) (pg 89). Each time the bearer fights, it makes 2 additional attacks with this weapon.

MELEE WEAPONS	RANGE	TYPE	S	AP	D	ABILITIES
Scissorhand	Melee	Melee	User	-2	1	Poisoned Weapon (4+) (pg 89). Each time the bearer fights, it makes 2 additional attacks with this weapon.
Shaimeshi blade	Melee	Melee	User	0	1	Poisoned Weapon (2+) (pg 89). Each time an attack is made with this weapon, if the target is not a VEHICLE unit, an unmodified wound roll of 6 inflicts 1 mortal wound on the target in addition to any normal damage.
Shardnet and impaler	Melee	Melee	User	-2	2	Each time the bearer fights, it makes 1 additional attack with this weapon.
Spirit-leech tentacles	Melee	Melee	User	-1	1	Each time an attack is made with this weapon, on an unmodified wound roll of 6, that attack has a Damage characteristic of 2.
Sslyth battle-blade	Melee	Melee	User	-2	1	-
Stunclaw	Melee	Melee	+1	0	2	Each time an attack is made with this weapon, an unmodified wound roll of 6 inflicts 1 mortal wound on the target in addition to any normal damage.
Talos ichor injector	Melee	Melee	-	-	-	Each time the bearer fights, no more than one attack can be made with this weapon. Each time an attack is made with this weapon, if a hit is scored, the target suffers D3 mortal wounds and the attack sequence ends.
Talos gauntlet	Melee	Melee	+2	-3	3	Each time an attack is made with this weapon, subtract 1 from that attack's hit roll.
Ur-Ghul talons	Melee	Melee	User	-1	1	-
Venom blade	Melee	Melee	User	-1	1	Poisoned Weapon (2+) (pg 89)
Wrack blades	Melee	Melee	User	-1	1	Poisoned Weapon (4+) (pg 89)

118

GLOSSARY

Below you will find a glossary that contains a number of terms used in this Codex.

WEAPONS AND WARGEAR

Any number of models can each have their Weapon A replaced with Weapon B: When this wargear option is selected for a unit, any number of models in that unit that are equipped with Weapon A can each have its weapon replaced with Weapon B. It is possible for only some of the models in that unit to have their weapon replaced and for others not to.

Splinter weapon (pg 116): A shard carbine, a ranged weapon whose profile includes the word 'splinter' or a Relic that replaces a splinter weapon.

Wych weapon: A category of weapons only used by Wyches or Succubus, or a Relic that replaces one of these weapons. A full list of Wych weapons can be found on page 116.

DETACHMENT TYPES

Drukhari Detachment (pg 49): A Detachment in which every unit (with the exception of **Unaligned** units) is a **Drukhari** unit.

Haemonculus Coven Detachment (pg 49): A **Drukhari** Detachment that has been designated as a Haemonculus Coven Detachment. Only **<Haemonculus Coven>** units can gain an Obsession in a Haemonculus Coven Detachment.

Kabal Detachment (pg 49): A **Drukhari** Detachment that has been designated as a Kabal Detachment. Only **<Kabal>** units can gain an Obsession in a Kabal Detachment.

Realspace Raid Detachment (pg 49): A **Drukhari** Detachment that has been designated as a Realspace Raid Detachment. All **Drukhari** units (with the exception of **Blades for Hire** units) can gain an Obsession in a Realspace Raid Detachment.

Wych Cult Detachment (pg 49): A **Drukhari** Detachment that has been designated as a Wych Cult Detachment. Only **<Wych Cult>** units can gain an Obsession in a Wych Cult Detachment.

UNIT UPGRADES

Lords of Commorragh (pg 50-51): Catch-all term for a series of upgrades that can be applied to Archons, Succubus and Haemonculus. Each gains a new keyword and access to a Kabalite Diversion, Wych Cult Spectacle or Haemonculus Proclivity. These grant the upgraded model a new ability and access to a new Warlord Trait and Relic, which can be selected for that model instead of any others they have access to.

Favoured Retinues (pg 52): Catch-all term for a series of upgrades that can be applied to Kabalite Warriors, Wyches and Wracks. Each gains a new keyword and a series of new abilities.

CRUSADE

Ascendant Lord Character (pg 80): One **Character** model in your Crusade army can be designated as your army's Ascendant Lord. They gain a new keyword and enable your army to gain Raid Spoils points.

Raid Spoils points (pg 80): A resource generated by Drukhari Crusade armies, commonly used to gain new territories for your Ascendant Lord (see above.)

Territories (pg 80): In Crusade, your **Ascendant Lord Character** unit can gain territories. These can be found on the Territories table on page 81. Additional abilities are gained once your Ascendant Lord has gained a certain number of territories, as detailed on page 82.

OTHER COMMON TERMS

Artefact of Cruelty (pg 74-75): A type of Relic that can be given to **Drukhari Character** models.

Kabal, Wych Cult or Haemonculus Coven Relics (pg 54-64): A series of Relics associated with one of the named Kabals, Wych Cults or Haemonculus Covens. These are only available to **Character** models that are part of that Kabal, Wych Cult or Haemonculus Coven.

Kabal, Wych Cult or Haemonculus Coven Warlord Traits (pg 54-64): A series of Warlord Traits associated with one of the named Kabals, Wych Cults or Haemonculus Covens. These are only available to **Character** models that are part of that Kabal, Wych Cult or Haemonculus Coven.

Raiding Forces (pg 49): Detachment ability for **Drukhari** Detachments.

Realspace Raid (pg 49): Detachment ability for **Drukhari** Detachments.

Stratagem label: A Stratagem's labels are written beneath its title and can include: Drukhari; Battle Tactic; Epic Deed, Strategic Ploy; Requisition; Wargear. A Stratagem can have more than one label; for example, a Stratagem with 'Drukhari – Wargear Stratagem' has both the Drukhari and Wargear labels.

Weakling Kin (pg 49): Detachment ability for **Drukhari** Detachments.

REFERENCE

Below you will find a bullet-pointed summary of several Drukhari rules.

BLADE ARTISTS (PG 89)

- Each time a model in this unit makes an attack with a melee weapon, on an unmodified wound roll of 6, improve the Armour Penetration characteristic of that attack by 1.

COMBAT DRUGS (PG 89)

- An ability primarily used by <**Wych Cult**> units.
- Before the battle, select one or randomly determine 2 abilities from the list for each unit with the Combat Drugs ability.
- If you have an army roster, these selections must be noted on it for each unit.

DETACHMENT ABILITIES (PG 49-65)

If an army is Battle-forged, units in **Drukhari** Detachments gain the following:

- **Drukhari** units gain the Realspace Raid, Raiding Forces and Weakling Kin abilities.
- **Drukhari** units gain Obsessions, as described as part of the Raiding Forces and Realspace Raid abilities.
- Troops units in **Drukhari** Detachments gain the Objective Secured ability (this ability is described in the Warhammer 40,000 Core Book).

INSENSIBLE TO PAIN (PG 89)

- Each time a model in this unit would lose a wound, roll one D6: on a 5+, that wound is not lost.

<Kabal>, <Wych Cult> AND <Haemonculus Coven> KEYWORDS (PG 88)

- When you include a unit with any of these keywords, nominate which Kabal, Wych Cult or Haemonculus Coven it is from.
- Replace every instance of the <**Kabal**>, <**Wych Cult**> or <**Haemonculus Coven**> keyword on that unit's datasheet with the name of your chosen Kabal, Wych Cult or Haemonculus Coven.

POISONED WEAPONS (PG 89)

- Many Drukhari weapons have the Poisoned Weapon ability. Such a weapon will have an ability that reads 'Poisoned Weapon' and then a value, such as (2+) or (4+).
- Each time an attack is made with a poisoned weapon against a unit (excluding **Vehicle** or **Titanic** units), an unmodified wound roll of this value is always successful.

POWER FROM PAIN (PG 89)

- Power From Pain only applies if every model in your army has the **Drukhari** keyword (excluding **Unaligned** models).
- Units with this ability gain the following abilities at the start of each battle round. These abilities are cumulative:
  - Battle Round 1: Models in this unit have a 6+ invulnerable save.
  - Battle Round 2: This unit is eligible to declare a charge in a turn in which they Advanced.
  - Battle Round 3: Each time a model in this unit makes a melee attack, add 1 to that attack's hit roll. If this unit has the **Vehicle** or **Monster** keyword, it does not suffer the penalty incurred to its hit rolls for firing Heavy weapons at enemy units that are within Engagement Range of it.
  - Battle Round 4: Models in this unit have a 5+ invulnerable save.
  - Battle Round 5+: Each time a Morale test is taken for this unit, it is automatically passed. If this unit's characteristics can change as it suffers damage, this unit is considered to have double the number of wounds remaining for the purposes of determining what those characteristics are.

RAID SPOILS POINTS(PG 80-83)

- Can be gained in a variety of ways while your Crusade Order of Battle contains a unit with the **Ascendant Lord** keyword.
- Can be spent on a variety of abilities to give bonuses to your Crusade army.